mari D'Alessandra

W9-CNU-729

A /Opinionated
VERY
MAP-GUIDE
to the Best of Everything
in the
BIG APPLE

BOOKS BY DAVID YEADON

WILD PLACES—A Journey Around the Earth (in progress)
NEW YORK'S NOOKS AND CRANNIES (revised: MacMillan, 1986)
SECLUDED ISLANDS OF THE ATLANTIC COAST (Crown, 1984)
FREE NEW YORK (Free City Books, 1982)
HIDDEN CORNERS OF BRITAIN (Geo. Allen & Unwin, W.W. Norton, 1981)
BACKROAD JOURNEYS OF SOUTHERN EUROPE (Harper & Row, 1981)
BACKROAD JOURNEYS OF THE WEST COAST STATES (Harper & Row, 1979)
WHEN THE EARTH WAS YOUNG (Doubleday, 1979)
NOOKS & CRANNIES OF NEW YORK CITY (Charles Scribner & Sons, 1979)
HIDDEN CORNERS OF THE MID-ATLANTIC STATES (Funk & Wagnall's, 1976)
HIDDEN CORNERS OF NEW ENGLAND (Funk & Wagnalls, 1976)
NEW YORK BOOK OF BARS, PUBS AND TAVERNS (Hawthorn, 1975)
SUMPTUOUS INDULGENCE ON A SHOESTRING—a cookbook (Hawthorn, 1974)
WINE TASTING IN CALIFORNIA (Camaro, 1973)
HIDDEN RESTAURANTS OF CALIFORNIA—2 vols. (Camaro, 1972)
EXPLORING SMALL TOWNS OF CALIFORNIA—2 vols. (Ward Ritchie, 1972)

Other Titles in Preparation:
- ★ **BOSTON: The Best Places**
- ★ **CHICAGO: The Best Places**
- ★ **LOS ANGELES: The Best Places**
- ★ **SAN FRANCISCO: The Best Places**
- ★ **LONDON: The Best Places**
- ★ **PARIS: The Best Places**

PERENNIAL LIBRARY

HARPER & ROW, PUBLISHERS, New York
Cambridge, Philadelphia, San Francisco, Washington
London, Mexico City, São Paulo, Singapore, Sydney

NEW★YORK

THE
BEST
PLACES

★

**DAVID
YEADON**
&
The Best Places Team

Designed by David Yeadon and Kevin Ullrich
Production by Jeanette Friedman
Typesetting by Batsch Spectracomp, Mechanicsburg, PA
Printed by Bookcrafters, Inc., Chelsea, MI
Typestyles: Clearface and Frutiger
FIRST EDITION

Library of Congress Data:
Yeadon, David.
New York : the best places.
Includes index.
1.New York, (N.Y.)—Description—1981- —
 Guide books. I.Title.
F128.18.Y398 1987 917.47'10443 86-45711
ISBN 0-06-096099- X (pbk.)

To Hugh Van Dusen
for his quiet patience, faith
and humor

CONTENTS

CONTENTS

INTRODUCTION

This small book is a celebration.

No other city in the world has the energy, the vibrancy, the variety and the sheer overwhelming array of excellences in so many areas of endeavor as New York today. In less than a decade, The Big Apple has burgeoned from near-bankruptcy into one of the fastest growing and most dynamic metropolitan areas in the nation. Renaissances flourish throughout many neighborhoods given up for lost a few years ago. A score of new restaurants open in Manhattan every week; new galleries, stores, hotels, office towers and apartment complexes mushroom as if by magic; the city glows with roaring new life, new confidence and a new sense of purpose.

What better time is there, then, for this modest celebration—a simply structured homage to the high standards and even higher aspirations which characterize the Big Apple's new blossoming? Our small guidebook features the very best, and only the best, offered by the city to residents and visitors alike.

New York: The Best Places is not just one more addition to an already remarkable procession of city guide books. The bookstore shelves are full of publications (including a few of my own) which cumulatively provide thousands of pages of descriptive reviews incorporating virtually every hotel, restaurant, museum, store and service on the island. Many of them are magnificent resources if you have the time and endurance to digest voluminous information and advice. But it's hard work!

Inspired originally by one of many impromptu requests from friends for short takes on "The Best Steakhouses" or "The Best Really Authentic Chinese Restaurants," I realized it was time to embark on the search for excellence and prepare formal and researched lists of the city's best offerings in a wide range of regularly used resources.

What seemed at first a rather straightforward process of compilation and elimination turned out to be a most strenuous undertaking which required team effort from colleagues and experts (see 'The Best Places Team'). Without their arduous contributions, this publication would have been virtually impossible.

While recognizing the dangers inherent in the elimination process, we hope our combined attempt has produced a practical, easy-to-use celebratory guide to the very best at the very best of times in the very best of cities. And if, through our labors, your life in or your visit to the Big Apple is enriched just a little, then we shall allow ourselves a single sigh of satisfaction before starting the process all over again for the next edition!

Enjoy.

David Yeadon

PRICE RANGE CODE:
INEXPENSIVE: Up to $15 without tips or drinks
MODERATE: $15-$30
EXPENSIVE: $30-$60
VERY EXPENSIVE:$60+

BEST PLACES TEAM

Incredibly, the simple, straightforward concept of "BEST PLACES" created heartburn, harassment and, at times, total havoc in the daily routines of its opinionated author and the members of his splendid support team. Their dedication to excellence and their belief in the project gave the work wings as they sought to lift themselves from all too familiar quagmires of confusion and despair. Without the support team's enthusiastic participation, it's doubtful the book would have materialized. And now—hardly pausing for breath, bouquets or balthasars of celebratory champagne—they begin the process all over again for next year's edition.

Special thanks to:

★ **Jeanette Friedman**, journalist, author and 'queen' of New York Nightlife, whose recent book, **New York Nights** (Free City Books, $5.95), is the first comprehensive after-dark guide to the world's most exciting metropolis. This super-mom of 4 transforms herself into 'The Flatbush Flash,' an energetic dynamo seeking out the very best the city has to offer—and then reduces everyone's mountains of notes and investigations into a manageable and meaningful format . . . the floppy disk.

★ **Walker Joyce**, playwright, actor, talk show host and film critic, has lived his entire life in or around the Big Apple and has no plans to go anywhere else—especially as he intends an immediate Broadway comeback. 'The Voice' will be remembered with affection by scores of individuals he interviewed during the course of the **BEST PLACES** project.

Thanks also go to many other team members whose contributions to the research and compilation process were invaluable:

Jo & Bob Blaine
Gene Cetrone
Juli D'Ambly
Hannelore Hahn
Carol Horn
Olga Herrara
Chef Mark of Jacqueline's
Maryellen Martin
Vincent Minuto
Leandra Mitucheri
Tim Noble
Martin Snyder
Jeff Stimpson
Tatiana Stoumen
Monica Beliveau Tobey

Most of all, our gratitude goes to the countless experts in the city, whose opinions and comments we sought throughout all phases of the project.

Thank you for your time and your uncompromising concern for quality and consistency of excellence in a city which deserves the title **Showcase of Excellence**.

THE
BEST
PLACES

TOP HOTELS

david yeadon ©

1 Helmsley Palace
455 Madison Ave. (bet. E.50th & E.51st Sts., 10022)/888-7000
Despite Mamma Leona's self-applauding ads, this fiefdom is
something to crow about. Don't miss touring the rooms of
The Villard Houses, which comprise this hostelry's glorious foundation and provide an Old World ambience as a res-
pite from the slick-city style of the new hotels.

2 Hotel Carlyle
35 E.76th St. (10021)/744-1600
It was the Kennedy address every time they came to town in
the Camelot days, and it's the great Bobby Short's now. Catch
him at the piano in the Café.

3 The Mayfair Regent
610 Park Ave. (at E.68th St., 10021)/288-0800
Understated and totally elegant ambience in oversized
rooms, plus afternoon tea in the lounge and **Le Cirque** is
right next door. Need we say more?

4 The Plaza Athenée
37 E.64th St. (10021)/734-9100
Utter luxury in this New York equivalent of the Paris original,
right down to the Louis XV decor-detail—and **Le Régence**
restaurant, too.

5 The Plaza Hotel
5th Ave. at 59th St. (10019)/759-3000
A wonderful grande dame with all the verve of Katie Hep-
burn. You need never leave the premises for fine dining and
dancing, and for dessert, go outside and hail a hansom cab
for a romantic ride through Central Park.

6 The Ritz-Carlton
112 Central Park So. (10019)/757-1900
There's an air of country estate here, especially in the fall,
which the song says is the best time of all. Cozy up to **The
Jockey Club Bar** and have one for us.

7 The St. Regis
2 E. 55th St. (10022)/753-4500
Its appointments, from the copper jewelbox which houses the
doorman to the Maxfield Parrish murals in the King Cole
Room, are impeccable, as are the catering service (headed by
former Gov. Carey's son, Chris) and the banquet staff.

8 The Sherry Netherland
781 5th Ave. (at E.59th St., 10022)/355-2800
The troupers and tourists from Tinseltown (the other coast)
seem to have colonized this confection of a co-op hotel. Might
it be the efficient and discreet staff that makes the difference?

9 The United Nations Plaza Hotel
1st Ave. (at E.44th St., 10017)/355-3400
This is truly a world class contemporary hotel with all the
international accoutrements, including the sounds of a thousand languages wafting through the mirrored halls (no tower
of Babel, this). The health club is exceptional, and the eastern view is a nice perk. There's even a harpist with your afternoon tea!

10 The Waldorf-Astoria
Park Ave. at E.50th St., (10022)/355-3000
A New York legend, truly venerable, from the poshest pub in
town (**The Bull & Bear**), the lobby with its cocktail terrace,
the ballrooms—all grand—and the boutiques with their international fashion imports, right down to the marble loos in the
lobby. Impressive, indeed.

MAJOR TOURIST ATTRACTIONS

W 106 St.
W 96 St.
W 86 St.
W 79 St.
W 72 St.
W 65 St.
W 59 St.
W 57 St.
W 50 St.
W 42 St.
W 34 St.
W 23 St.

E 110 St.
E 106 St.
E 96 St.
E 86 St.
E 79 St.
E 72 St.
E 65 St.
E 59 St.
E 57 St.
E 50 St.
E 42 St.
E 34 St.
E 23 St.

West End Ave.
Riverside Dr.
Broadway
Amsterdam
Columbus
Central Park West
5 Ave.
Madison
Park
Lexington
3 Ave.
2 Ave.
1 Ave.
York Ave.

CENTRAL PARK

Broadway

Lincoln Tunnel

11 Ave.
10 Ave.
9 Ave.
8 Ave.
7 Ave.
6 Ave.
5 Ave.
Madison
Park
Lexington
3 Ave.
2 Ave.
1 Ave.

Queensborough Br.
Queens - Midtown Tun.

EAST RIVER
FDR Drive

W 14 St.
Greenwich
Hudson
7 Ave. S.
Bleecker
Spring
Canal

E 14 St.
Ave. A
St. Marks Pl.
Houston
Bowery
Delancey
Williamsburg Br.
Broadway
East Broadway

HUDSON RIVER

Holland Tunnel

Chambers
Wall

Manhattan Br.
Brooklyn Br.
Fulton

Brooklyn Battery Tunnel

david yeadon ©

(4)
(2)
(6)
(3)
(5)

1 The Circle Line
W.42nd St. at the Hudson River/563-3200
May-November/usually every hour/Adults $12; children under 12
$6

It's a shame more native New Yorkers don't avail themselves of this option and others in this category. Julie Eisen's "liners" around the island and the tour guides rattle off the highlights along the way. The Day Line division (279-5151) steams upriver to Bear Mountain and West Point in summers.

2 The Empire State Building
350 5th Ave. (W.34th St. & 5th Ave.)/736-3100
Daily 9:30 a.m.-midnight/Adults $3; children under 12 $1.75

This is still the most incredibly beautiful art deco monument on the planet, and the architectural details are amazing. You might say this is the male version of the species, with the Chrysler Building at E.42nd and Lexington as its female mate. Both buildings are magnificent and richly endowed with city folklore.

3 The New York Stock Exchange
20 Broad St. (at Wall St.)/656-3000
M-F 9:30 a.m.-3:30 p.m./Free

This is the oldest part of town and is very rich, historically as well as financially. Here's where the fat cats play their high money stakes games and the brokers fight for seats (which are not easy to get) and develop ulcers, while the rest of us dabble. Around the corner is Federal Hall, where Georgie said goodbye.

4 Rockefeller Center *see CONTEMPORARY LANDMARKS*
from W.47th-W.51st Sts., from 5th-6th Aves.

An urban planner's dream. The underground concourse is a maze of shops, boutiques and corridors that run even farther afield than the aboveground complex. NBC, the grand old lady of TV, offers tours here, too, as does Radio City, home of the Rockettes and the world's largest pipe organ. Call 489-2074 for details on tours.

5 The Statue of Liberty
Battery Park and Whitehall St./363-3200
Daily 9-4/$1 at the Statue

You could take a ritual 25çen ride on the Staten Island ferry, but if you take the ferry to Liberty Island,(Adults $3.25, children under 12 $1.50) you will be overwhelmed by the magnificent restoration of this great symbol of America as melting pot. If your grandparents came here from across the ocean, you'll find a piece of your heritage here. If you're a Mayflower type, you'll learn about the rest of us.

6 The South Street Seaport *see CHILDRENS'*
PLEASURES

7 World Trade Center
Church & Liberty Sts./466-7377
Observation Deck (Tower 2) open 9:30-9:30/Adults $2.95; children 6-12 $1.50

While architectural critics will argue forever over the aesthetic merits of these twin 110 story towers rising above the 5 acre plaza and underground shopping complex, visitors will soar to the 107th floor of 2 World Trade Center and remember the Rooftop Promenade for the rest of their lives. Splurgers will go on to sip and snack at the **Hors d'Oeuvrerie**, dance and dine at **Windows on the World** or enjoy the fabulous 7-course set dinner with wines at **Cellar in the Sky**. Even the most jaded of tourists will return to earth lighter in spirit (and wallet).

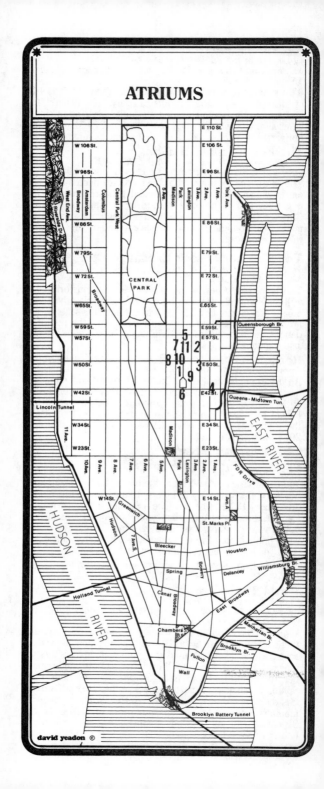

ATRIUMS

1 Chemcourt
277 Park Ave. (bet. E.47th & E.48th Sts.)
This enormous spaceframe greenhouse, recently added to the Chemical Bank Building, contains a wealth of lush greenery, exotic blossoms, plus a marble waterfall, snack bars and nibbling niches—even a lunchtime concert area!

2 Citicorp Center—The Market
E.53rd St. & Lexington Ave./559-4259
Three busy levels of stores, restaurants, gourmet shops and snack bars, plus a daily abundance of concerts, shows and entertainments. St. Pete's church offers free jazz. (935-2200).

3 Crystal Pavillion
E.50th St. at 3rd Ave.
Exotically ultra-modern, multilevel setting, with live music, restaurants, chic stores and public seating. Friendly—not frigid.

4 Ford Foundation
320 E.42nd St. (bet. 1st & 2nd Aves.)
One of the city's best contemporary landmarks (see listing), built around a 100-foot high atrium jungle of full-sized trees, streams and a pond. Benches would be nice.

5 Galleria
115 E.57th St. (bet. Park and Lexington Aves.)
One of the first modern atriums in the city, and it still features lunchtime concerts on Tuesdays and Fridays and a piano bar in the evenings.

6 Grand Central Terminal
E.42nd St. & Park Ave.
Overwhelmingly spacious interior, which is surprisingly restrained under a celestial ceiling, with continuous live human theatre and free Wednesday tours (935-3960). A must-see, as is the atrium of the Grand Hyatt next door.

7 IBM Garden
590 Madison Ave. (at E.57th St.)
A vast serene bamboo-shaded court (the bamboo grows to 50 feet, at least), with plenty of public seating, occasional Wednesday concerts and an excellent science and arts gallery.

8 Olympic Tower
5th Ave. & E.51st St./371-8100/935-2220
This Aristotle Onassis creation provides a sophisticated store-lined arcade between streets and a seating area alongside the waterfall, greenery galore and Thursday evening concerts.

9 Park Ave. Atrium
66 Lexington Ave. (bet. E.45th & E.46th Sts.)
An awesome 23-story interior space with glass elevator and an enormous 245-foot sculpture of Winged Gamma.

O Park Ave. Plaza
55 E.52nd St. (bet. Madison & Park Aves.)
An innovative, "squeezed-in" tower over the Racquet and Tennis Club, with lush plant life, waterfall, café and more in a chromed and columned setting.

1 Trump Tower
725 5th Ave. (bet. E.56th & E.57th Sts.)
Like it or not, Donald outdid the rest, with this 6-story extravagance of pink marble, bronze mirrors, exotica, orchids galore and uniformed doormen, as well as exclusive boutiques and shops with top names.

CHILDREN'S PLEASURES

Map labels:

E 110 St.
E 106 St.
E 96 St.
W 106 St.
W 96 St.
W 86 St.
E 86 St.
W 79 St.
E 79 St.
W 72 St.
E 72 St.
W 65 St.
E.65 St.
W 59 St.
E 59 St.
W 57 St.
E 57 St.
W 50 St.
E 50 St.
W 42 St.
E 42 St.
W 34 St.
E 34 St.
W 23 St.
E 23 St.
W 14 St.
E 14 St.

West End Ave.
Riverside Dr.
Amsterdam
Broadway
Columbus
Central Park West
5 Ave.
Madison
Park
Lexington
3 Ave.
2 Ave.
1 Ave.
York Ave.

CENTRAL PARK

Queensborough Br.
Queens - Midtown Tun.
Lincoln Tunnel
11 Ave.
10 Ave.
9 Ave.
8 Ave.
7 Ave.
6 Ave.
5 Ave.
Park
Lexington
3 Ave.
2 Ave.

EAST RIVER
FDR Drive

Ave. A
Greenwich
Hudson
7 Ave. S.
St. Marks Pl.
Bleecker
Houston
Bowery
Delancey
Williamsburg Br.
Spring
Canal
Broadway
East Broadway
Holland Tunnel
HUDSON RIVER
Chambers
Manhattan Br.
Brooklyn Br.
Fulton
Wall
Brooklyn Battery Tunnel

Madison

david yeadon ©

The Bronx Zoo
185th St. & Kaysmiroff Blvd. (The Bronx)/367-1010/220-5100
One of the finest zoos in America, you can bring the kids for an entire day and still not get to see all of it. Amazing bird and reptile houses, wonderous exhibits, and a view in the monkey house of the world's most dangerous creature. Can you guess what it is?

Brooklyn Children's Museum
145 Brooklyn Ave. (at St. Marks' Pl.), Brooklyn/1-718-735-4400
They love kids here, and it shows in the hands-on exhibits and the wide variety of special programs. We refuse to grow up, and keep going back.

Children's Museum of Manhattan
Manhattan Laboratory Museum
314 W.54th St. (bet. 8th & 9th Aves.)/765-5904
Midtown's answer to the aforementioned. They too believe in roll-up-your-sleeves and hands-on experiences. The nature and art opportunities (and so many others, too) are top-notch.

Museum of Holography
11 Mercer St. (north of Canal St.)/925-0526
You and your youngsters will be spellbound by this new-fangled, 3-D artform; dozens of images, including a pretty girl who blows you a kiss, suspended in thin air at this SoHo nook.

Naturemax Theatre
At the Museum of Natural History
Central Park West at W.79th St./873-1300
The schedule changes as do the feature films, so call ahead and start weaning your youths from the usual Hollywood teen trash via this cinema's striking educational fare. The offerings include "The Dream Is Alive," which chronicles the space shuttle program, and others of similar ilk.

New York City Transit Authority Exhibit
Schermerhorn St. and Boerum Pl., Brooklyn/718-330-3060
A clever and nostalgic assemblage of New York history as depicted by its public transportation systems. Everything from 19th century trolleys to subway cars, models galore and all very hands-on. Accomplishes the virtually impossible by evoking affection for the MTA! Great PR!

The New York Experience
The McGraw-Hill Building
1221 6th Ave. (bet. W.48th & W.49th Sts.)/869-0345
A 60-minute, multimedia depiction of Gotham's history, from its inception to the present. Be prepared for popping Nathan Hales and other surprises, and don't panic when the room fills with smoke. It's all part of the experience which delights all ages.

The South Street Seaport
Between Water and John Sts. at the East River/669-9424
Though we frankly prefer the Rouses' more laudatory restorations in Baltimore and Boston, this development is worthy and welcome. Start with the "Seaport Experience" (similar in idea to "The NY Experience") and try to get the kids to concentrate on history instead of glitz, which is reserved for grown-ups later in the evening. Then move through the gastronomic displays and surprises of The Market and Pier 17, the towering clippers and sailing ships. Great place! (If you arrive in the very early morning, you'll enjoy the redolent reality of the Fulton St. Fishmarket, too).

CONTEMPORARY LANDMARKS

Note: In spite of regular surges of development and billions of real-estate investment dollars, Manhattan continues to to be plagued by overwhelmingly mediocre architecture (narcotechture, gimmicktechture, maudlinmodular, and instant slums). The following, however, are worthy of note and the section on atriums includes additional candidates. But we still need the NY equivalent of the Pompidou Center and Plaza in Paris, a better appreciation of our waterfront potentials and much, much more. Battery City, we hope, will lead the way.

1 Citicorp Center/see also ATRIUMS
Hugh Stubbins & Associates, 1978
Lexington Ave. (bet. E.53rd & E.54th Sts.)
Stylishly urbane and one of the most active atriums in town.

2 88 Pine Street
I.M. Pei, 1974
Bet. Water & Front Sts.
Pristine, unpretentious architecture in the form of a pure white waterfront tower. A reminder of clear contemporary values.

3 Ford Foundation/see also ATRIUMS
Kevin Roche, John Dinkledoo and Associate, 1967
320 E.42nd St. (bet. 1st & 2nd Aves.)
An understated surprise combination of offices and a fine interior garden atrium.

4 Guggenheim Museum/see also MAJOR MUSEUMS
Frank Lloyd Wright, 1959
5th Ave. bet. E.88th & E.89th Sts.
Forever a shrine to the master and one of the world's most exciting contemporary interiors.

5 Lever House
Skidmore, Owings & Merrill, 1952
390 Park Ave. (bet. E.53rd & E.54th Sts.)
One of the innovative pioneers left standing, but may soon suffer the wreckers' ball. Very ahead of its time, it's the epitome of curtain wall construction. Ditto the Seagram Building next door.

6 Police Headquarters
Gruzen & Partners, 1973
Bet. New, Henry & Pearl Sts., (off Park Row)
A bold brick cube in one of the city's best new civic spaces, just off Foley Square. Lovely lunching spot in summertime.

7 Rockefeller Center
Reinhard, Hofmeister and others, 1931-40
From W.48th-W.51st Sts., bordered by 5th & 6th Aves.
Perfect example of integrated civic design, with parklets, walkways, plazas, ice rink, cafés, shops and more in a setting of soaring limestone towers. This town has forgotten how it's done when done right. We hope someone remembers soon.

8 The United Nations Building
An International Committee of Architects, 1952
1st Ave. bet. E.42nd-E.48th Sts.
Amazing result of uncluttered civic design (it came from a committee!) on a unified site. There are quaint aspects, but it's still a subtle massing of shapes amplified by Dinkledoo's One United Nations Plaza,a green glass gem next door.

9 Whitney Museum of American Art
Marcel Breuer and Hamilton Smith, 1966
Madison Ave. & E.75th St.
An aggressive, arrogant statement in granite and concrete expressing bold contempt for mealymouthed traditionalists, as does the art displayed within.

FREE INDOOR ACTIVITIES

E 110 St.
W 106 St.   E 106 St.
W 96 St.   E 96 St.
West End Ave.   Broadway   Amsterdam   Columbus   Central Park West   5 Ave.   Madison   Park   Lexington   3 Ave.   2 Ave.   1 Ave.   York Ave.
W 86 St.   E 86 St.
W 79 St.   E 79 St.
CENTRAL PARK
W 72 St.   E 72 St.
W 65 St.   Broadway   E 65 St.
W 59 St.   E 59 St.   Queensborough Br.
W 57 St.   E 57 St.
④
W 50 St.   ③   E 50 St.
②   ⑥
W 42 St.   E 42 St.   Queens - Midtown Tun.
Lincoln Tunnel
W 34 St.   E 34 St.   EAST RIVER
11 Ave.   W 23 St.   E 23 St.
10 Ave.   9 Ave.   8 Ave.   7 Ave.   6 Ave.   5 Ave.   Madison   Park   Lexington   3 Ave.   2 Ave.   1 Ave.   FDR Drive
W 14 St.   E 14 St.   Ave. A
HUDSON   Greenwich   St. Marks Pl.
Hudson   7 Ave. S.   ①
Bleecker   Houston
Spring   Bowery   Delancey   ⑤   Williamsburg Br.
Canal   Broadway
Holland Tunnel   East Broadway
RIVER   Chambers   Manhattan Br.
Fulton   Brooklyn Br.
Wall
Brooklyn Battery Tunnel

david yeadon ©

Citicorp Center—*a daily array of pleasures see ATRIUMS*

Columbia University *see FREE ACADEMIC ACTIVITIES*

1 Cooper Union
3rd Ave. at E.7th St./254-6300

A wide range of mostly free public events during the academic year in this renowed 127-year-old establishment on the East Village fringe. Most popular are the 8 p.m. weekday lectures, concerts and readings, plus inexpensive courses. A calendar is a must.

Grand Central Terminal Tour *see ATRIUMS*

2 New Dramatists' Workshop
424 W.44th St. (bet. 9th & 10th Aves.)/757-6960

Hotbed of new theatre, with free lunchtime workshops (Tu-Th at 12:30) and some performances at 7:30 weekdays. Call for reservations.

New York Public Libraries *see LIBRARIES*
Call 221-7676 for complete events calendar/869-8089 for exhibition information/661-7220

An amazing line-up of freebies: lectures, films, concerts, children's programming, jazz, readings, etc.

The New York Stock Exchange *see TOURIST ATTRACTIONS*

3 St. Peter's Church
619 Lexington Ave. at E.54th St./935-2200

Free lunch theatre, usually on Tuesdays from noon, Oct.-May. *see FREE INDOOR CONCERTS*

4 Vidal Sasoon
767 5th Ave. (at E.59th St.)/535-9200

Still continuing their freebie hair cuts by trainees for selected clients. Call 223-9177 for details.

5 Shapiro's Winery
126 Rivington St. (bet. Norfolk & Essex Sts.)/674-4404

Not exactly a pristine Napa Valley Winery, but certainly a novel introduction to the making of 25 varieties of kosher wine—and they let you taste, too. Sundays 11-4. (A neat diversion if you're shopping on the Lower East Side.)

Frank Silvera Workshop
317 W.12.5th St. (off St. Nicholas Ave.)/662-8463

Free play readings and productions by lesser-knowns, usually on Mondays at 7:30 and Saturdays at 3.

TV Shows

Free TV show tickets can usually be obtained from the Convention and Visitor's Bureau at 2 Columbus Circle (397-8222) and from sidewalk hawkers around Rockefeller Center. Also, you can call local networks for tickets. Could be for game shows, new sitcoms or specials. Sometimes all you do is watch. At others, you're part of the laugh-track input or you're asked to fill out opinion forms. Usually lots of fun.

The United Nations
1st Ave. (bet. E.45th & E.49th Sts./754-7713/1234

In spite of constant criticism of its political activities (or lack of them) it's still a fascinating experience, either as a self-conducted tour with the booklet, the guided tour, or with free tickets to observe The General Assembly (Tower of Babel, anyone?). Monday-Friday 10-3.
see TOURIST ATTRACTIONS

FREE OUTDOOR ACTIVITIES

CENTRAL PARK

HUDSON RIVER

EAST RIVER

FDR Drive

Queensborough Br.

Queens - Midtown Tun.

Lincoln Tunnel

Holland Tunnel

Williamsburg Br.

Manhattan Br.

Brooklyn Br.

Brooklyn Battery Tunnel

Riverside Dr.
West End Ave.
Broadway
Amsterdam
Columbus
Central Park West
5 Ave.
Madison
Park
Lexington
3 Ave.
2 Ave.
1 Ave.
York Ave.

11 Ave.
10 Ave.
9 Ave.
8 Ave.
7 Ave.
6 Ave.
5 Ave.
Madison
Park
Lexington
3 Ave.
2 Ave.
1 Ave.

Broadway

Greenwich
Hudson
7 Ave. S.
Bleecker
Bowery
Houston
Spring
Delancey
Canal
Broadway
East Broadway
Chambers
St. Marks Pl.

E 110 St.
E 106 St.
E 96 St.
E 86 St.
E 79 St.
E 72 St.
E 65 St.
E 59 St.
E 57 St.
E 50 St.
E 42 St.
E 34 St.
E 23 St.
E 14 St.

W 106 St.
W 96 St.
W 86 St.
W 79 St.
W 72 St.
W 65 St.
W 59 St.
W 57 St.
W 50 St.
W 42 St.
W 34 St.
W 23 St.
W 14 St.

david yeadon ©

Bronx Zoo
185th St & Kaysmiroff Blvd./367-1010
O.K., so we cheat a little—but this is one of NY's most fascinating experiences and it's all free on Tuesdays, Wednesdays and Thursdays—so go!

Bryant Park *see PARKS & GARDENS*

1 Central Park
Call the magic numbers, 397-3156/755-4100, for an abundance of concerts, storytellings, ice skating and Urban Ranger Walks (360-8194). Get them to send you the monthly freebie catalogue.

2 City Hall Park
Regular outdoor lunchtime concerts, Urban Ranger Walks, and a free tour of City Hall.

3 Dag Hammerskjold Plaza
2nd Ave. at E.47th St./661-0033
Great for lunch, with or without free concerts. Pick the right time, and you might even become a newsmaker on this favorite corner during political protests and demonstrations.

4 Exxon Park
W.49th-W.50th Sts. (bet. 6th & 7th Aves.)./489-4306
A hidden urban delight, with free summer lunchtime concerts on Tuesdays & Thursdays.

5 Federal Hall National Memorial
Wall & Broad Sts./264-8711
Daily colonial folksongs in the rotunda and Wednesday lunchtime classical concerts at 12:30.

6 International Paper Plaza
77 W.45th St. (at 6th Ave.)/536-5968
A shadowed plaza with abundant seats for concerts and theatre lunches on Mondays, Wednesdays and Fridays during summertime.

7 St. Marks Park
E.10th & 2nd Ave./397-3192
Free lunchtime snacks and noon concerts in the shaded burial ground at the reincarnated church.

South St. Seaport *see CHILDREN'S PLEASURES*

8 Trinity Church Gardens
74 Trinity Pl. (at Wall St. & Broadway)/285-0800
A lovely mellow niche for summertime lunch concerts—arranged and impromptu.

9 Upper Plaza
55 Water St.
East River views and summer lunchtime concerts on the Downtown Canyon fringe.

Washington Square *see PARKS & GARDENS*

0 The World Trade Center
Liberty, West & Church Sts./466-7377/466-4170
Excellent outdoor concerts and entertainments, especially on Wednesday lunchtimes during summer.

HIDDEN ENCLAVES

david yeadon ©

1 Chelsea
9th Ave. & W.22nd St.
This is the hub of an historic district, surrounded by an unusual collection of 19th century wooden buildings, Federal townhouses and the General Theological Seminary at Chelsea Square. Quite lovely.

2 Grove Court
10 Grove St. at Hudson St.
A row of mid-19th century workers' cottages in a delightfully tranquil court full of shade and birdsong. Nearby on Bedford St. is the odd "Twin Peaks" and the tiny Edna St. Vincent Millay House (9.5'wide). A magic corner in the heart of the Village.

Morris-Jumel Mansion
W.160th St. at Edgecombe Ave./923-8008
Secluded historic museum, once the home of Aaron Burr's wife and yet another HQ for Gen. George; lovely views of garden, and don't miss the adjoining Sylvan Terrace.

3 Paley Park
E.53rd St. at 5th Ave.
A popular lunchtime niche among the monoliths. Complete with waterfall, trees, tables, chairs and a snack booth, it's ideal for a summer day or people-watching. Also try nearby **Greenacre Park** on E.51st St. between 2nd & 3rd Aves.

4 Patchin Place
6th Ave. at W.10th St.
Dainty, shaded cul-de-sac of 19th century worker's cottages which later served as homes for Theodore Dreiser, Eugene O'Neill and e.e. cummings. Unchanged and easy to miss.

5 Pomander Walk
Links W.94th & W.95th Sts. bet. Broadway & West End Ave.
This link between two busy streets is a film-set replica of a narrow English "walk", with Tudor gables, flower boxes, trimmed hedges and Anglophile residents. Very quaint.

6 St. John's in The Village
Waverly Pl. at W.11th St./243-6192 for hours
Through the office and out the door is this charming oasis. Also visit the nearby secluded garden of **St. Luke's-in-the-Fields** at Hudson bet. Barrow & Christopher Sts.

7 Sniffen Court
E.36th St. (bet. Lexington & 3rd Aves.)
A lovely surprise in the form of a series of converted coach houses and stables with brimming flower boxes, climbing plants, gaslights and brass trimmings. Home to artists, actors and architects. Lovely for sketching.

8 Tudor City
E.42nd St. (off 1st & 2nd Aves.)
Odd Elizabethan and Tudor-trimmed towers peering down on quiet parks and gardens, the East River and the U.N. complex. Affectionately idiosyncratic.

9 Washington Mews
North of Washington Square (bet. University Pl. & 5th Ave.)
An almost Mediterranean setting of cobbled walks, pastel colored cottages, abundant vines and treasured tranquility behind iron gates. Another ideal location for sketching.

HISTORIC LANDMARKS
see also UNUSUAL LANDMARKS

1 City Hall, 1802-1812
Park Row & Broadway
McComb & Mangin's French classical plan with Federal accents. Much restored and still elegant, overlooking a delightfully shady park. Governor's room with authentic furnishings is open M-F 10-3

2 Cooper-Hewitt Museum, 1901/*see also MAJOR MUSEUMS 2 E.91st St.*
Andrew Carnegie's austere chateau, an outstanding reminder of New York's glory days and now serves as a museum of design.

3 Federal Hall Memorial, 1842
Nassau & Wall Sts./264-8711
One of the city's finest examples of Greek Revival edifices couched in the canyons of the downtown financial district. George Washington took his oath of office on this site in 1789 and now there's a small museum plus free summer concerts. When they all moved to Philly, the building fell down, so the pieces were sold for salvage, and the present structure was erected.

4 Grand Central Terminal, 1913/*see also ATRIUMS*
An overwhelming spatial experience within a powerful Beaux Arts structure topped by Jules Couteau's sculpture of classical deities (plus the American eagle).

5 The New York Public Library, 1911/*see LIBRARIES/OUTDOOR SCULPTURE*
Revered by architects as New York's prime expression of the Beaux Arts tradition, adorned with superb Roman detailing and guarded by those famous felines.

6 The Old Downtown Police Headquarters, 1909
Centre St. bet. Grand & Broome Sts.
An often-ignored Renaissance Revival masterpiece buried in grit, grime and grunge on the edge of Little Italy. Needs help.

7 Trinity Church, 1846
Broadway & Wall Sts.
An unforgettable black silhouette, holding its own gracefully against the burgeoning towers of contemporary commerce, offering summer solace, solitude, comfort, concerts and more to the weary Wall St. workers. Call 285-0872 for details.

8 U.S. Customs House, 1907
Whitehall St. at Bowling Green
Cass Gilbert's Beaux Arts bonanza with brilliant counterpoints in Daniel Chester French's sculptures representing four continents, and Reginald Marsh's 1937 murals in the vast rotunda.

9 The Villard Houses
The Helmsley Palace Hotel/Madison Ave. bet. E.50th & E.51st Sts.
Now forming the main entrance and elegant public rooms of the Helmsley Palace, Henry Villards magnificent Italian Renaissance houses retain their external quietude and interior elegance. Well worth a visit—and don't miss the Urban Center in the north wing.

10 The Woolworth Building, 1913 *see LOBBIES.*
233 Broadway (bet. Park Pl. & Barclay St.)
A $13 million dollar (in those days) Cathedral of Commerce and the world's tallest building until 1930.

LOBBIES
see ATRIUMS and HISTORIC LANDMARKS

1 AT&T, 1917 headquarters
195 Broadway (bet. Dey & Fulton Sts.)

An overpowering array of enormous Doric columns bathed in a haunting pink and cream light. Certainly idiosyncratic and ideal for games of hide & seek.

2 Bowery Savings Bank, 1894
130 Bowery (bet. Broome & Grand Sts.)

A majestic Beaux Arts creation by McKim, Mead & White (our favorites, who have left their mark all over the city) in a part of town not known for its architectural extravagance; the supporting Corinthian columns are graced by the great skylight dome.

3 Bowery Savings Bank, 1923
110 E.42nd St. (bet. Park and Lexington Aves.)

An elaborate Romanesque basilica with 70-foot columns done in a myriad of marbles and carvings, presumably extolling the virtues of wealth. Enervating and humbling at the same time!

4 Chanin Building, 1929
E.42nd St. & Lexington Ave. SW

Almost next door, an enthusiastic celebration of art deco tinged with Gothic flourishes. Note the ornate convector grilles, elevator doors and bas-relief mailboxes set in a profusion of polished Istrian marble.

5 Chrysler Building, 1930
E.42nd St. & Lexington Ave. NE

Inside you'll discover a classic art deco creation in chrome steel and African marble providing the perfect setting for Edward Trumbell's vast transportation mural. Externally, one of the city's most beloved skyscraper spires.

6 Cunard Building, 1921
25 Broadway at Morris St.

Wonderful extravaganza of terracotta and tiled arches, nymphs, dolphins, Neptune and denizens of the deep, plus Ezra Winter's early explorers' murals, tumultuously depicting Leif Eriksson, The Vikings, Columbus and even Sir Francis Drake. Unfortunately, this is now a post office and sadly in need of restoration.

7 The Daily News Building, 1930
220 E.42nd St. (bet. 2nd & 3rd Aves.)

The world's largest rotating globe and succinct time and space statistics, surrounded by wall displays of famous front-page banner headlines, serve to remind us of our insignificance in the vast scheme of things.

8 The Hall of Records, 1911
31 Chambers St. (at Centre St.)

Like most of our civic spaces, this could do with a face lift. Rejoice anyway in the operatic exuberance of the central hall.

9 The Woolworth Building
233 Broadway (bet. Park Pl. and Barclay St.)

Cass Gilbert's splendid romp of gargoyles, bas-reliefs, filigreed wrought iron and mosaics, in a mystically-lit 3 story lobby which both overwhelms and titillates. There's even a brochure to reveal the intricacies.

MAJOR MUSEUMS

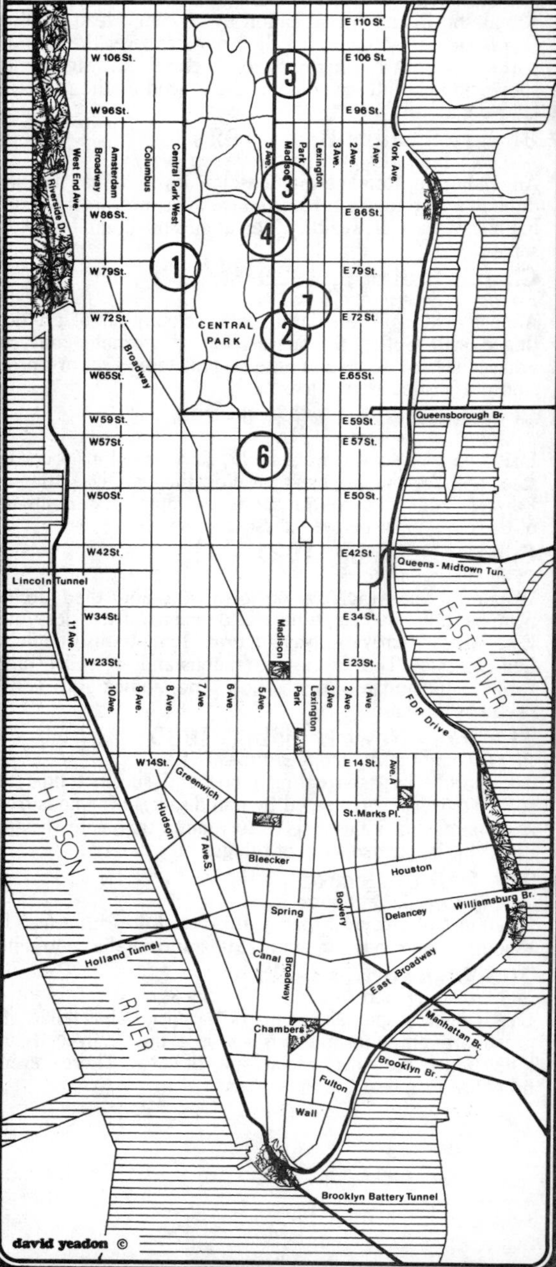

W 106 St.
W 96St.
E 110 St.
E 106 St.
E 96 St.

⑤

Riverside Dr.
West End Ave.
Amsterdam
Broadway
Columbus
Central Park West

5 Ave.
Madison
Park
Lexington
3 Ave.
2 Ave.
1 Ave.
York Ave.

③
④

W 86 St.
E 86 St.

①

W 79 St.
E 79 St.

⑦

②

W 72 St.
CENTRAL PARK
E 72 St.

Broadway

W 65St.
E 65 St.

W 59 St.
E 59 St.
Queensborough Br.

W 57 St.
E 57 St.

⑥

W 50 St.
E 50 St.

W 42 St.
E 42 St.

Lincoln Tunnel
Queens - Midtown Tun.

11 Ave.
10 Ave.
9 Ave.
8 Ave.
7 Ave.
6 Ave.
5 Ave.
Park
Lexington
3 Ave.
2 Ave.
1 Ave.
Ave. A

W 34 St.
E 34 St.
EAST RIVER

W 23 St.
E 23 St.

FDR Drive

W 14 St.
E 14 St.

Greenwich
St. Marks Pl.

HUDSON
Hudson
7 Ave. S.
Bleecker
Houston

Spring
Bowery
Delancey
Williamsburg Br.

Holland Tunnel
Canal
Broadway
East Broadway

RIVER
Chambers
Manhattan Br.

Brooklyn Br.
Fulton

Wall

Brooklyn Battery Tunnel

david yeadon ©

1 American Museum of Natural History
Central Park West at W.79th St./873-1300
M-S 10-4:45, W & F to 9, Su 11-5/contribution
These stately halls have always been our epitome of a real museum, and this one defines nature from the dinosaur age on. (The enormous skeletal bulk of these creatures still sends shivers up and down spines!) **The Hayden Planetarium**, 873-8828, is one of the neglected entertainment options in town.

The Cloisters
Fort Tryon Park/T-Su 10-4:45, Su noon-4:45/923-3700/ contribution
Whole rooms and monastic cloisters from Europe have been imported and restored lovingly, thanks to the Rockefellers. Now they're filled with medieval artworks selected and curated by the Metropolitan Museum of Art. Incredibly non-New York, especially the daily Gregorian chant concerts in the gardens.

2 The Frick Collection
1 E.70th St. (at 5th Ave.)/288-0700/T-S 10-6, Su 1-6/Adults $2, Su $3; children 50¢
This is one of the last remaining mansions along Fifth Avenue built during the Robber Baron Era. Still used as a residence by the Frick family, the splendor of 18th and 19th century art is overwhelming. Explore this home with its exceptional collection of masterpieces spanning centuries and forget yourself at the reflecting pool on a rainy afternoon.

3 The Guggenheim Museum
1071 5th Ave. (at E.88th St.)/360-3500/W-Su 11-5, T 'til 8/Adults $3.50; students $2
Be ready for the spiraling ramp and the contemporary artworks on display at this hallmark Frank Lloyd Wright exhibition space. Whether you love it or hate it, it's definitely New York.

4 The Metropolitan Museum of Art
5th Ave. at E.82nd St./879-5000/T 10-8:45, W-S 10:4:45, Su 11-4:45/contribution
535-77/0
The largest jewel in New York's crown; an encyclopedic array of humankind's proudest creations is housed in this ornate revival building that seems to go on forever, with period rooms, knights in shining armor and more. Two of our favorites are The Temple of Dendur and John La Farge's mural-sized painting of Joan of Arc and her "voices."

5 Museum of the City of New York
1220 5th Ave. (off E.103rd St.)/534-1672/T-S 10-5, Su 1-5/Free
A fascinating cavalcade of the city's history, from New Amsterdam days to the present. We're particularly fond of the period rooms.

6 Museum of Modern Art
11 W.53rd St. (off 5th Ave.)/708-9500/T-Su 11-6, Th till 9/cl. W/ Adults $5; students $3.50, Th contribution
Indisputably the greatest collection of contemporary artworks under one roof. The first advocate of film as art, this institution's motion picture archive is a trove to be treasured.

7 The Whitney Museum of American Art
945 Madison Ave. (at E.70th St.)/570-3676/T-S 11-6, Su noon-6/ Adults $4; students & children free/T eves Free
The finest assortment of contemporary sculptures and paintings this side of MOMA. Gertrude Whitney, a scion of the Vanderbilt family, was the patron saint here, spending her money on treasures, not taxes!

OVERLOOKED MUSEUMS I

david yeadon ©

1 The Abigail Adams Smith Museum
421 E.61st St. (bet. 1st and York Aves.)/838-6878
M-F 10-4/Adults $2, children under 12, free
Hidden among the sterile towers behind stone walls, this tiny 9-room carriage house was built in 1799 for President John Adams' daughter, Abigail. A secluded gem surrounded by tranquil gardens.

2 The Dog Museum of America
51 Madison Ave. (bet. E.26th & E.27th Sts.)/695-8350
T-S 10-5, W till 7/contribution
This delightful and unexpected surprise is in the magnificent lobby of the New York Life Insurance Company and features small but fascinating exhibits on man's best and best-loved friend.

3 Forbes Galleries
Forbes Building, 60 5th Ave. (at W.12th St.)/206-5548/4448
T-S 10-4 (Th group tours only)/Free
As much a mixture of tastes and interests as Malcolm himself—toy soldiers, model boats, war art, famous historical manuscripts and of course, those fabulous Fabergé eggs!

4 IBM Gallery
Madison Ave. at E.56th St./407-6100
T-F 11-6, S 10-5/Free
Six shows featuring aspects of science, the arts and computer technology are held here every year. It's one of the loveliest lobbies in town, shaded by an enormous bamboo forest.

5 Museum of Broadcasting
1 E.53rd St. (off 5th Ave.)/752-7684
W-S noon-5, T till 8/Adults $3, children $1.50
Wonderful! A too-small repository of 60 years' worth of radio and TV programs with a 70 seat theatre and "on-demand" console entertainment. Well worth it.

6 Nicholas Roerich Museum
319 W.107th St. (bet. Broadway & Riverside Dr.)/864-7752
T-S 2-5/Free
Richly evocative artworks by the mystic-painter-writer, with a community gallery and chamber music recitals mid-month on Sundays at 3 p.m. Unusual and provocative.

7 Old Merchant's House *see SPOOKY SPOTS*
29 E.4th St. (bet. Lafayette St. and The
Bowery)/777-1089/Sundays only 1-4/Adults $2, children Free
An evocation of mid-19th century life in New York at the home of the wealthy hardware merchant, Seabury Tredwell. Quite, quite charming.

8 Theodore Roosevelt's Birthplace
28 E.20th St./260-1616/W-Su 1-5/Adults 50¢; children Free
An initmate townhouse bursting with exhibits and displays of Roosevelt memorabilia, plus free chamber music concerts on Saturday at 2. Inviting, even for nonfans of Teddy.

9 The Ukrainian Museum
203 2nd Ave. (at E.12th St.)/228-0110/W-Su 1-5/Adults $1, children Free
Colorful collections of Ukrainian folk costumes, art, ceramics and famous handpainted eggs—"pyansky." Different and diverting.

OVERLOOKED MUSEUMS II

W 106 St.
W 96 St.
W 86 St.
W 79 St.
W 72 St.
W 65 St.
W 59 St.
W 57 St.
W 50 St.
W 42 St.
W 34 St.
W 23 St.
W 14 St.

E 110 St.
E 106 St.
E 96 St.
E 86 St.
E 79 St.
E 72 St.
E 65 St.
E 59 St.
E 57 St.
E 50 St.
E 42 St.
E 34 St.
E 23 St.
E 14 St.

Riverside Dr.
West End Ave.
Amsterdam
Broadway
Columbus
Central Park West

Central Park

Park
Madison
Lexington
3 Ave.
2 Ave.
1 Ave.
York Ave.

Queensborough Br.

Lincoln Tunnel
11 Ave.
10 Ave.
9 Ave.
8 Ave.
7 Ave.
6 Ave.
5 Ave.
Park
Madison
Lexington
3 Ave.
2 Ave.
1 Ave.

Queens - Midtown Tun.

EAST RIVER
FDR Drive

Greenwich
Hudson
7 Ave.S.
Bleecker
Spring
Canal
Broadway

Ave. A
St. Marks Pl.
Houston
Bowery
Delancey
East Broadway

Williamsburg Br.

HUDSON
RIVER

Holland Tunnel

Chambers
Fulton
Wall

Manhattan Br.
Brooklyn Br.

Brooklyn Battery Tunnel

david yeadon ©

1 The Air and Space Museum
Pier 86, foot of W.46th St./245-0072/W-Su 10-5/Adults $4.75; children $2.50

The Intrepid, grand old lady of the fleet, is a veritable and venerable historical repository for our Navy's last 44 years. Come learn of her storied service, from WWII to VietNam to NASA.

2 The American Craft Museum
40 W.53rd St./956-3535/T-Su 10-5 p.m./Adults $3.50; children under 12 Free

The works of over 4000 native and foreign-born artisans in clay, glass, fiber, wood, metal and other media. Period clothing is also lovingly displayed.

The Brooklyn Museum
200 Eastern Parkway, Brooklyn/718-638-5000/783-3077/W-S 10-5, Su noon-5/Adults $3; students and seniors $1.50

A supreme collection of Egyptian art in the western hemisphere. There's a wonderful collection of John Singer Sargent watercolors, sculptures by Frederic Remington, some outstanding Bierstadts, an excellent decorative arts department with a heavy emphasis on city history, and a Prints and Drawing department that won't quit. The gift shop also carries items that the museum is de-accessioning. One of the seven best in the whole of America.

3 The Cooper-Hewitt Museum
5th Ave. at 91st St./860-6898/Su noon-5, T 10-9, W-S till 5/Adults $3; students and seniors $1.50

Andrew Carnegie's vast mansion now houses one of finest collections of fabrics and textiles, designer gowns from the rich and famous, architectural drawings and decorative arts.

4 The Jewish Museum
1109 5th Ave. (at E.92nd St.)/860-1888/M-Th noon-5, Su 11-6/ Adults $2; children $2 (Free Tues. 5-9)

Much of the collection comes from the pre-war Dresden Jews, who realized what the Nazis were about to do and shipped all their valuable heirlooms to NY for safekeeping. There's a 19th century mansion hidden behind the contemporary façade.

5 The New York Historical Society
170 Central Park West (at W.77th St.)/873-3400/T-F 11-5, S 10-5, Su 1-5/Adults $2; children $1

This second oldest museum in America has some of the loveliest paintings, lithographs and pop culture remnants anywhere. Their huge library and morgue of local newspapers are priceless assets. The building isn't half bad, either — a beautiful 19th century granite masterpiece left over from West Side Mansion days.

6 The Pierpont Morgan Library
29 E.36th St./685-0008/T-S 10:30-5, Su 1-5/contribution

This is more than just one of the finest libraries in America. It's also a museum in its own right, ensconced behind beautiful wrought-iron gates and plush greenery. You'll find treasures like an original Gutenberg Bible and autographed copies of Shakespeare's folios. These priceless items were easily affordable for a man who once bailed out the U.S. Treasury, and was one of the original robber barons who ruled the city social scene.

OUTDOOR SCULPTURE

1 Alice in Wonderland (1959)
Conservatory Walk in Central Park (off 5th Ave. and E.74th St.)
Polished by a million or more tiny hands & feet, this José de Creeft creation, overlooking the boating pond, is one of the city's most utilized sculptures, with George Lorber's Hans Christian Andersen looking on from nearby. (Free children's stories on Saturdays at 11 a.m., May-Sept.). The Delacorte Musical Clock at the zoo is only a short stroll away.

2 Bethesda Fountain (1875)
The North End of the Mall, Central Park Lake
Emma Stebbins' glorious centerpiece of the once-elegant terrace with the winged Angel of the Waters bestowing grace on four portly cherubs (Temperance, Peace, Purity and Health). Best on non-boombox days.

3 Cube (1973)
140 Broadway (Liberty & Cedar Sts.)
Isamu Noguchi's scarlet cube, balanced on one corner and pieced by a cylindrical shaft, generates stop action tension against the dark and refined passiveness of Skidmore, Owings & Merrill's Marine Midland Bank.

4 Farragut Memorial (1880)
Madison Square and E.24th St. (off 5th Ave.)
A major creation of Augustus Saint-Gaudens enhanced by Stanford White's masterful setting—a classic combination of grace, power & melancholia. Worthy studying.

5 Four Trees (1972)
One Chase Manhattan Plaza (bet. Pine, Liberty, Nassau & William Sts.)
Dubuffet's delightful, towering white fantasy of black-outlined overlapping shapes offering woodsy shade on this otherwise dreary raised plaza.

6 Lions (1912)
The New York Public Library (W.42nd St & 5th Ave.)
In white and regal glory, these two splendid guardians of the gates are New York's most loved sculptures. "Patience" and "Fortitude" are brought to us thanks to the talents of Edward Clark Potter.

7 Reclining Figure (1969)
Lincoln Center, Broadway & W.64th St.
The bold massing and rough textures of Henry Moore's powerful figure contrast effectively with Eero Saarinen's Vivian Beaumont Theatre and the sickly-slickness of the other neoclassical edifices.

8 Theodore Roosevelt Memorial (1936)
American Museum of Natural History (Central Park West at W.79th St.)
Admirably pompous and full of the conceit of young America, James Earl Fraser's work impresses, amuses or irritates. Decide for yourself.

9 Untermeyer Memorial Fountain (1947)
Central Park Conservatory Gardens (5th Ave. at 105th St.)
A wondrous little world of arbors, rosebuds, bowers and blossoms surrounds this exquisite fountain and its frolicking nymphs behind the elaborate wrought-iron gates. Thank you, Walter Schott.

PARKS & GARDENS

W 106 St.
W 96 St.
W 86 St.
W 79 St.
W 72 St.
W 65 St.
W 59 St.
W 57 St.
W 50 St.
W 42 St.
W 34 St.
W 23 St.
W 14 St.

E 110 St.
E 106 St.
E 96 St.
E 86 St.
E 79 St.
E 72 St.
E 65 St.
E 59 St.
E 57 St.
E 50 St.
E 42 St.
E 34 St.
E 23 St.
E 14 St.

West End Ave.
Riverside Dr.
Amsterdam
Broadway
Columbus
Central Park West

Central Park

5 Ave.
Madison
Park
Lexington
3 Ave.
2 Ave.
1 Ave.
York Ave.

CENTRAL PARK

Broadway

11 Ave.
10 Ave.
9 Ave.
8 Ave.
7 Ave.
6 Ave.
5 Ave.
Madison

Lincoln Tunnel

Queensborough Br.
Queens - Midtown Tun.

EAST RIVER
FDR Drive

Ave. A
St. Marks Pl.

Greenwich
Hudson
7 Ave. S.
Bleecker

Houston
Bowery
Spring
Delancey
Canal Broadway
East Broadway
Williamsburg Br.

HUDSON

RIVER

Holland Tunnel

Chambers
Fulton
Wall
Manhattan Br.
Brooklyn Br.

Brooklyn Battery Tunnel

david yeadon ©

1 Battery Park
State St. & Battery Place
Far more than a simple port for the harbor ferries, the park offers 22 acres of greensward for the weary, with fine sculptures, cozy niches and that cute green and white fireboat house. At the northern end is the delightfully shaded Bowling Green.

2 Bryant Park
W.40-W.42nd Sts., bet. 5th & 6th Aves.
The recent sweeps by police and renovation of the park has restored it to its rightful place as a mellow haven for those who work in the area. Behind the NY Public Library, it's now a safe haven to lunch, people-watch, snack,snooze, browse through the book stalls or enjoy a wealth of free summer concerts and entertainments.

3 Carl Schurz Park
E.84th-E.89th Sts., East End Ave.-East River
A wonderful tree-filled enclave with fine river views and sneaky peeps into the grounds of Gracie Mansion, the Mayor's official residence. The John Finley Walk overlooking the East River has a raised boardwalk south to 80th St..

4 Central Park Surprise
5th Ave. at E.105th St.
The mother of them all—glorious Central Park—possesses a little-known secluded gem, The Conservatory Gardens.
see OUTDOOR SCULPTURE

Fort Tryon Park
192nd & Dyckman Sts., from Broadway to Riverside Drive.
Yet one more Rockefeller gift to the city, in the form of 62 acres of wooded hills overlooking Inwood and the Hudson River. Remnants of 1776's Fort Washington, exotic flower gardens, and The Cloisters Museum make this a unique place apart in the city.

5 Gramercy Park
Lexington Ave. (bet. E.21st-22nd Sts.)
Although access is limited to key holders (residents of buildings overlooking the square), this whole historic district is a summer-stroll delight, encompassing "Block Beautiful" (E.19th St. bet. 3rd Ave. & Irving Pl.) The National Arts Club and the immortal **Pete's Tavern**.
see LITERARY WATERING HOLES

6 Tompkins Square
E.7th-E.10th Sts., Aves. A-B
A fascinating funky mélange of East Village yuppies, punks and Ukrainian residents in this large shady park, surrounded by renovated brownstones, galleries and some very odd and popular bar-restaurants.

7 Union Square
E.14th-E.17th Sts., bet. Park Ave. So. & Broadway
Yet one more recent transformation to this square, that has seen it all from the Knickerbocker Society and Communist marches, to the rise and fall of S. Klein, and the return of famous publishing houses. It's now a safe, sophisticated focus for a rapidly improving neighborhood.

8 Washington Square
Southern end of 5th Ave.
Once a place of execution and ignominious burial, now one of the most beloved centers of impromptu entertainment, people-watching and urban adventure that just never seems to stop. When you're here, you're home.

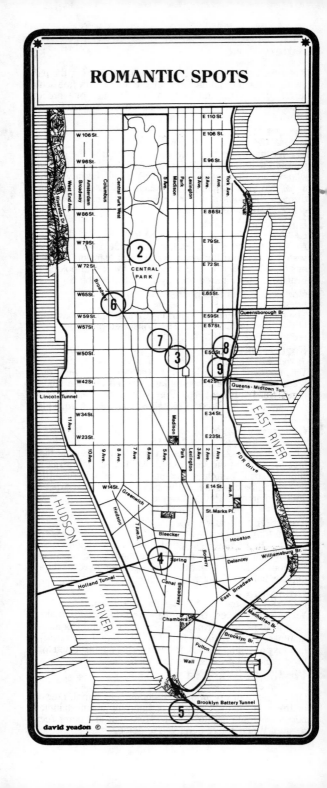

ROMANTIC SPOTS

E 110 St.
E 106 St.
E 96 St.
E 86 St.
E 79 St.
E 72 St.
E 65 St.
E 59 St.
E 57 St.
E 50 St.
E 42 St.

W 106 St.
W 96 St.
W 86 St.
W 79 St.
W 72 St.
W 65 St.
W 59 St.
W 57 St.
W 50 St.
W 42 St.
W 34 St.
W 23 St.
W 14 St.
E 34 St.
E 23 St.
E 14 St.

West End Ave.
Riverside Dr.
Broadway
Amsterdam
Columbus
Central Park West
5 Ave.
Madison
Park
Lexington
3 Ave.
2 Ave.
1 Ave.
York Ave.

CENTRAL PARK

Lincoln Tunnel
Queensborough Br.
Queens - Midtown Tun.

11 Ave.
10 Ave.
9 Ave.
8 Ave.
7 Ave.
6 Ave.
5 Ave.
Park
Lexington
3 Ave.
2 Ave.
1 Ave.
Ave. A
Madison

FDR Drive

EAST RIVER

HUDSON RIVER

Greenwich
St. Marks Pl.
7 Ave. S.
Hudson
Bleecker
Houston
Bowery
Spring
Delancey
Williamsburg Br.
Holland Tunnel
Canal
Broadway
East Broadway
Chambers
Manhattan Br.
Brooklyn Br.
Fulton
Wall
Brooklyn Battery Tunnel

david yeadon ©

Here's our oddball assortment of favorite cozy and dallying niches around town. Go find your own. See also ROMANTIC RESTAURANTS, DINING & DANCING/HIDDEN ENCLAVES/PARKS & GARDENS

Abigail Adams Smith Museum
see OVERLOOKED MUSEUMS

Battery Park by the Little Firehouse
see PARKS & GARDENS

1 Brooklyn Heights Esplanade
Overlooks the East River (bet. Orange and Remsen Sts.)
One of the best anytime walks in the 5 boroughs, with magnificent vistas of Manhattan and optional (and expensive) supper at the River Café, too! (Water St. at the East River).

2 Central Park *see PARKS & GARDENS*
One of the world's most romantic places, especially the Conservatory Garden, Belvedere Castle, The Wollman Memorial Rink, and Strawberry Fields—best of all, do it in a horsedrawn carriage.

The Cloisters & Fort Tryon Park
see MAJOR MUSEUMS/JOGGING ROUTES

3 Helmsley Palace Hotel
Madison Ave. At E.50th St./888-7000
Not too much kiss 'n' cuddle in the public places, but perfect for the prelude—an almost too extravagant revival of the Villard Houses.

John Finley Walk *see PARKS & GARDENS*

Morris-Jumel Mansion *see HIDDEN ENCLAVES*

Pomander Walk *see HIDDEN ENCLAVES*

Roosevelt Island *see JOGGING ROUTES*

4 SoHo Galleries
Pick a warm summer evening and become part of West Broadway's tumultuous scene, gallery and restaurant-hopping all the way from Grand to Houston and the all side streets in between.

South Street Seaport *see CHILDREN'S PLEASURES*
Perfect for proposals

5 Staten Island Ferry *South Ferry*
Also perfect for proposals.

6 Top of the Park
Gulf & Western Building, W.60th St. & Central Park West
Classic views of Central Park in settings of Old World charm.

7 Top of the Sixes
666 5th Ave. (at W.53rd St.)/757-6662
A magnificent view, in spite of narrow windows, and you'll be treated with Old World grace for the price of a drink.

8 Top of The Tower/Mitchell Place
Mitchell Pl. at 1st Ave. (at E.49th St.)/355-7300
A classic cocktail lounge overlooking the jeweled and rubied canyons, where motion is discernible and you can sense the city's lifeblood.

9 The United Nations Garden
1st Ave. bet. E.42nd & E.48th Sts.
A beautiful and usually secluded park overlooking the East River with little shady niches, including the hidden memorial to Eleanor Roosevelt.

World Yacht Club *see ROMANTIC RESTAURANTS*
If you get a proposal here, you're in trouble!

SPOOKY SPOTS

david yeadon ©

1 The Dakota Apartments
1 W.72th St. (at Central Park West)

Its very appearance—towering, brooding, full of shuttered windows and dark gables, made it an ideal setting for two popular chiller-thrillers, **Time and Again** and **Rosemary's Baby**. Then there was that tragic day in December of 1980, when John Lennon was gunned down at the entrance on W.72nd St. A sad and creepy place indeed.

2 Hotel des Artistes
1 W.67th St.

Author Margaret Widdemer reported that her apartment here had a strange presence which manifested itself through odd noises, doors opening and closing by themselves, and the inducement of instant paranoia in visitors. Psychics sensed the tormented spirit of a young girl on the winding staircase. Perhaps it was the essence of a previous tenant's daughter. . .a madwoman who had been sent to die in an insane asylum.

Morris-Jumel Mansion
Edgecombe Ave. at W.160th St.

This was Washington's headquarters during the Battle of Harlem Heights in 1776. Apparently one of his aides still walks the floors here, but we wonder who the woman is, seen walking with him.

3 Old Merchant's House
29 E.4th St. (bet. Lafayette St. & The Bowery)

On a winter's day, if you try, you may see the apparition of a beautiful girl garbed in 19th century finery above the fireplace on the third floor. Her name is Gertrude, reputed to be the winsome daughter of the house's original owner, Seabury Tredwell. He doomed her to spinsterhood when he exiled her only suitor (shades of Henry James).

4 The Player's Club
16 Gramercy Park So. (bet. Irving Pl. & Park Ave. So.)

During the gaslight era, this lovely theatrical fraternity was home to Edwin Booth. The best American classical actor of the 1800s, Booth never recovered, emotionally and professionally after his brother, John Wilkes, assassinated Abraham Lincoln. Edwin died in the top floor bedroom, which is left exactly as it was when he departed this mortal coil. Club manager Richard McBain gave us a tour. . .and while we didn't see anything, we hear that many staffers refuse to enter the chamber.

5 12 Gay Street
Off Waverly at 6th Ave.

Once upon a time the owner of this house was working into the wee hours of the morning when he was overcome by the scent of violets. Hearing footsteps in the entranceway he looked up, and beheld a figure of a man in formal clothes and Inverness cape. As he approached, the figure vanished "like a puff of smoke." Perhaps he was a patron of the opium den which originally held the premises, or a friend of former owner, Mayor Jimmy Walker. But then, he may also have been a participant in a rumored decapitation/murder which happened here. Or maybe. . .

STREET ENTERTAINMENTS

david yeadon ©

Note: Manhattan rejoices in ceaseless creativity; it's the world's biggest showcase of free acts and entertainments. Everywhere you look there are guitarists, chamber groups, magicians, mime artists and fast-buck street salesmen. Marvelous!

1 Battery Park Area
State St. & Battery Pl.

On a warm summer weekend, Battery Park is a riot of performers and laid-back listeners, and on weekday lunchtimes, the madness prevails and spreads north to encompass Bowling Green, Wall Street, Trinity Church and the steps of Federal Hall. Even money-hungry downtowners find times between deals for these delightful diversions.

Bryant Park *see PARKS & GARDENS*

2 Central Park
Mainly the Mall near 72nd St.

Who needs Broadway with this wealth of talent lined up sideshow-fashion along the Mall (and anywhere else crowds collect)? Just about the full range here from 12-piece steel bands to Archie's performing dogs!

3 5th Avenue
From St. Patrick's Cathedral to Central Park

A fascinating mix of entertainers (including a beautiful harpist on 55th St.), plus sidewalk salesmen galore.

4 Metropolitan Museum of Art
5th Ave. at E.82nd St.

It may have been unintentional but the steps and the plazas on either side of the majestic museum entrance provide perfect showcase spaces for top-flight street acts.

5 New York Public Library
5th Ave. & E.42nd St.

The steps at the main branch of the New York Public Library on 42nd St. & 5th Ave. are a perfect amphitheater, where offerings are similar to those at the Met and of equal caliber, plus the latest in street corner preachers covering every kooky kraze in town.

6 South Street Seaport

Down by the East River, at Peck Slip, it's almost too much. The summer crush often crowds out the performers, but there's always fun anyway (no matter what the more staid NYorkers say). The free **Summerpier** shows are an excellent bonus.

Street Bazaars (Bizarres?)

These and other instant sidewalk markets pop up and become a staple feature of the inner city, and keep going from early spring to late fall.

★ *14th St. from Broadway to 7th Ave.—the stores pour onto the sidewalks.*
★ *Astor Place—great for books & records*
★ *Ave.A at E.8th St., along the west edge of Tompkins Square.*
★ *Canal St. between W.Broadway and Lafayette St.*
★ *6th Ave. around W.4th St.—usually good for jewelry*
★ *6th Ave. at W.53rd St. for imported folk art*

7 Theatre District

All around Times Square, the quality of impromptu entertainment for matinee and evening crowds varies as much as does the quality of the Broadway productions themselves. Still worth watching, though.

Washington Square *see JOGGING ROUTES/PARKS & GARDENS*

UNUSUAL LANDMARKS

Map labels:

E 110 St.
E 106 St.
W 106 St.
W 96 St.
E 96 St.
Central Park West
Columbus
Amsterdam
Broadway
West End Ave.
Riverside Dr.
Park
Madison
Lexington
3 Ave.
2 Ave.
1 Ave.
York Ave.
5 Ave.
E 86 St.
W 86St.
W 79 St.
E 79 St.
W 72 St.
E 72 St.
CENTRAL PARK
W 65St.
E.65 St.
Broadway
W 59 St.
E 59 St.
Queensborough Br.
W 57 St.
E 57 St.
E 50 St.
W 50St.
E 42 St.
W 42St.
Queens - Midtown Tun.
Lincoln Tunnel
E 34 St.
W 34 St.
11 Ave.
EAST RIVER
E 23 St.
W 23St.
Madison
Park
Lexington
2 Ave.
1 Ave.
FOR Drive
10 Ave.
9 Ave.
8 Ave.
7 Ave.
6 Ave.
5 Ave.
W 14 St.
E 14 St.
Ave. A
Greenwich
Hudson
7 Ave. S.
St. Marks Pl.
Bleecker
Houston
Spring
Bowery
Delancey
Williamsburg Br.
HUDSON
RIVER
Canal
Broadway
East Broadway
Holland Tunnel
Chambers
Manhattan Br.
Brooklyn Br.
Fulton
Wall
Brooklyn Battery Tunnel

david yeadon ©

The Abigail Adams House (1799)
See OVERLOOKED MUSEUMS I

1 The Ansonia Hotel, 1904
2109 Broadway (bet. W.73rd & W.74th Sts.)
A joyous exuberance of extravagant Baroque detailing, fluttering about a soaring white confection. Once a haven for the rich and famous, now a little frayed at the edges.

2 Chelsea Hotel, 1884
222 W.23rd St. (bet. 7th & 8th Aves.)
A newly restored shimmering façade of ornate iron balconies against 12 stories of red and white Victoriana. Once a home away from home for literati, it became a dive for rock stars in the '70s—Sid Vicious did Nancy in here.

3 City Center of Music and Drama, 1924
135 W.55th St. (bet. 6th & 7th Aves.)
Custom-built for the Ancient and Accepted Order of The Mystic Shrine, this domed essay in architectural idiosyncracies is now the home of the City Center Ballet. It also closely resembles **The Town Hall** on W.43rd St, which may have been designed during the same period.

The Cloisters *see MAJOR MUSEUMS*
Romance and culture in total harmony.

The Dakota Apartments *see SPOOKY SPOTS*

The Dyckman House 1783
4881 Broadway (at W.204th St.)
A lovely little Dutch farmhouse, once commonplace around town in the old days. (Very few remain. There's the **Lefferts Homestead** in Prospect Park, and Brooklyn College has the pieces of the Ditmas Homestead that was removed 2-3 decades ago for the Student Center.) This one has a rose-adorned porch and is perched in a rocky garden. Authentically furnished, it's open to the public from T-Su 11-5. Well-worth the trek to the northernmost tip of the island, and it's free.

4 The Flatiron Building, 1902
175 5th Ave. (at E.23rd St. & Madison Square Park)
One of the town's most memorable skyscrapers, it sits on a triangle and is shaped like one. (It gave new definition to the corner office, especially on the north side.) Abundantly decorated with French renaissance details, rococo rosettes and more to fill out the flatness.

Jefferson Market Library, 1877 *see LIBRARIES*

Morris-Jumel Mansion, 1765 *see SPOOKY SPOTS*

5 The New York Yacht Club, 1899
37 W.44th St. (off 5th Ave.)
Go just for the windows. Magnificent old Galleon features.

6 St. Nicholas Cathedral, 1902
15 E.97th St. (off 5th Ave.)
A romp of Russian Orthodox detailing topped with five (yes, five) marvelous onion-shaped domes (just like in Moscow). While you're in the area, you might also want to check out the fantasy-façade of the Squadron A Armory on Madison and E.95th St.

7 Vanished Glories
6th Ave. bet. W.18th & W.23rd Sts.
These are the shells of glorious turn-of-century department stores which once lined the avenue. The elegance of the cast iron facades exceeds those in SoHo.

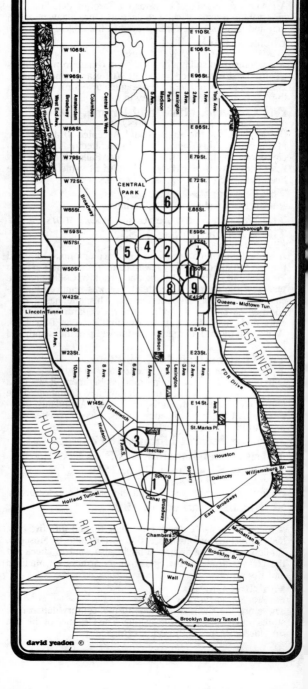

THE TOP TEN RESTAURANTS

*Note: While some may balk at seeing **Lutèce** and **Palm** on the same list, we believe that excellence comes in many quises.*

1 Chantarelle see FRENCH RESTAURANTS

2 The Four Seasons
99 E.52nd St. (at Park Ave.)/754-9494
Very expensive/M-S noon-2, 5-11:15/cl. Su/all major
This bastion of fine American-Continental cuisine is really two top spots in one: The Grill Room–site of power lunches–and The Pool Room, one of the most lushly romantic spaces in the NY restaurant realm. The menu and paintings change with the seasons, befitting the name. Game, fish and that wonderful sirloin tartare are the mainstays and everything is done with taste and panache and without overt snobbery. Out-of-towners receive the same respect as regulars—rather unusual in New York.

3 Il Mulino see ITALIAN RESTAURANTS

4 La Côte Basque
5 E.55th St. (off 5th Ave.)/688-6525
Very expensive/M-S noon-2:30, 6-10:15/cl. Su/all major cards
Henry Soulé's original dining room is one of the prettiest and most original in town. We love the rustic beams that rise overhead and Bernard Lamotte's murals, especially the St. Jean-de-Lux harbor scene, are experiences all by themselves. And the French fare here is on the city's honor roll; even the humble cassoulet rises to new heights. We're scallop hounds (among many other things) and they also do some very creative, delicious things with these nuggets. Wonderful place.

5 Le Bernardin see SEAFOOD RESTAURANTS

6 Le Cirque
58 E.65th St. (bet. Madison & Park Aves.)/794-9292
Very expensive/M-S noon-3, 6-10:30/cl. Su/Amex, CB, DC
Proprietor Sirio Maccioni seems to have guaranteed his superchic spot a permanent place in the pantheon. From the elegant, intimate setting to the classic cuisine to the elite patrons, it's a legendary leader of the pack. Kudos for the modest prix-fixe lunch and the city's best crème brûlée.

7 Lutèce
249 E.50th St. (bet. 2nd & 3rd Aves.)/752-2225
Very expensive/T-F noon-2, 6-10 (M&S dinner only)/cl. Su/Amex, CB, DC
Usually conceded to be the best eatery in New York, but don't be intimidated, however, for this most exclusive of dining rooms is actually very friendly. Situated in a lovely old brownstone, it retains its 19th century homey atmosphere. André Soltner probably collects more compliments than any other toque-wearer in town, so trust in his imagination and sample his "dégustation du chef." He'll expect a full critique, too!

8 The Oyster Bar see SEAFOOD RESTAURANTS

9 Palm see STEAK HOUSES

10 The Quilted Giraffe
955 2nd Ave. (bet. E.50th & E.51st Sts.)/753-5355
Very expensive/M-F 5:45-10/cl. S & Su/Amex, MC, V
In the stratosphere, meanwhile, another nouvelle specialist weighs in as a winner in the most expensive poll, and frankly we don't think it's justifiable, but who are we to argue with success? You could blow a whole week's salary on one bottle of wine, but ordering one of the innovative entrees without a sip of something from the sommelier would be gastronomic coitus interruptus!

AMERICAN RESTAURANTS
Also see STEAK HOUSES & SEAFOOD RESTAURANTS

david yeadon ©

1 American Harvest
Vista International Hotel,World Trade Center/938-9100
Expensive/M-F noon-2:30, M-S 6-10/all major
A rarity in the form of a notable hotel restaurant with monthly celebrations of regional cuisines. Intimate, but slightly intimidating clubby setting.

2 An American Place
969 Lexington Ave. (bet.E.70th & E.71st St.)/517-7660
Very expensive/6-10:30, cl. Su, res. req./all major
James Beard was the mentor of owner-chef Larry Forgione, and the master's touch can be discerned in this small, exciting place. Occasionally eccentric in its interpretations, but never boring.

3 Arcadia
21 E.62nd St. (off 5th Ave.)/223-2900
Very expensive/res. req./Amex, MC, V
Very in, very noisy at Ann Rosensweig's and Ken Aretsky's creation. For all the hype, there's great attention to quality, detail, plus honest and powerfully flavored innovations, and even a dinner seating for pre-theatre goers.

4 Bud's
359 Columbus Ave. (at W.77th St.)/724-2100
Very expensive/Su brunch noon-5:30, dinner till 8:30, M-S 6-11/ Amex, CB, DC
The West Side version of Jonathan Waxman's **Jams**, a simple, sensual setting for California cuisines, including eclectic salads, excellent calamari, and a unique American version of bouillabaisse.

The Four Seasons *see THE TOP 10 RESTAURANTS*

5 Gotham Bar & Grill
12 E.12th St./620-4020
Expensive/M-S 6-11, Su 5-10/all major
In spite of now familiar sophisti-neutral decor,which seems to be the trademark of new places on the 5th Ave. spine (from Washington Square to 23rd St.), Chef Albert Portaly creates high excitement with panache for wealthy pasta peckers and power brokers seeking peace.

6 Hubert's
102 E.22nd St. (bet. Lexington & Park Aves.)/673-3711
Very expensive/M-F noon-1:30, M-S dinner 6-10, cl. Su/Amex, MC, V
Precious little haven for admirers of nouvelle cuisine, including a reinvention of traditional New World favorites like New England Chowder and catfish "crisps."

7 Jams
154 E.79th St. (bet. Lexington & 3rd Ave.)/772-6800
Very expensive/T-F noon-12:30, dinner M-Th 6-11, F&S 6-11:30, Su 6-10/all major
An occasionally uneven and noisy but rarely uninteresting LA flavored haven for the chic-to-chic crowd, offering a mix of almost-traditional and downright-different creations.

8 Jezebel
630 9th Ave. at W.45th St./582-1045
Moderate/6-midnight, cl. Su/Amex
A candidate for our unusual category, this almost Victorian jungle-bordello-flavored concoction is matched by equally unconventionally attired staff who serve remarkably authentic soul food right down to the spoonbread & grits.

Quilted Giraffe *see TOP TEN RESTAURANTS*

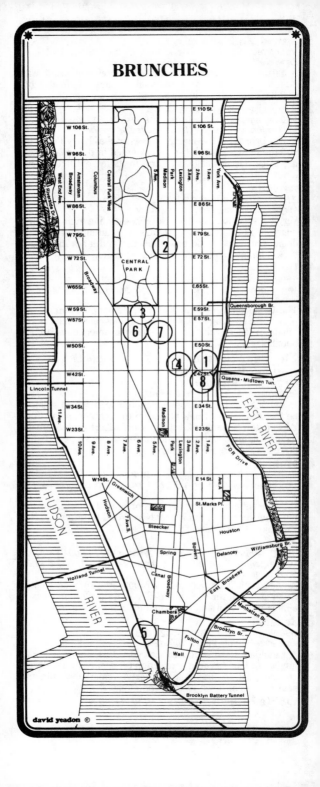

BRUNCHES

Note: We've selected the groaning-board buffet-style Sunday brunches. So, choose your mood, take your pick and make reservations.

Ambassador Grill
United Nations Plaza Hotel/1st Ave. at E.44th St./355-3400
$33 per person/2 sittings: 11:30 & 1:45/all major
An utterly elegant environment made more so by the piano music, liberal pourings of champagne for the international power-brokers and those lovely lobsters at the buffet.

Café Carlyle
The Carlyle Hotel/35 E.76th St. (off Madison Ave.)/744-1600
$25.75 per person/2 sittings: noon & 2 p.m./all major
Refined European atmosphere (home of beloved pianist Bobby Short) and sumptuous buffet to bring joy to the most jaded of palates. Drinks are additional.

Café de la Paix
St. Moritz Hotel/50 Central Park South /755-5800
$26.50 per person/from 11:30-3:30/all major
A glorious spread brimming with mounds of cold shrimp, clouds of poached salmon, pâtés, hot dishes and huge roasts—all this and a view of Central Park, too. One cocktail included.

Crystal Fountain
Grand Hyatt Hotel/E.42nd St. at Lexington Ave./883-1234
$23.95/10:30-3/all major
Soaring fountain and high-society ambience for "theme" Sunday brunches (Cajun, Paris, Oktoberfest, etc.). Lovely idea. Lovely spread. Drinks not included.

Hors D'Oeuvrerie
Windows on the World/1 World Trade Center/938-1111
$19.95/noon-7:30/all major
Nothing could be finer than to eat above most diners in the early afternoon—and you can't get much higher than this for a lofty international buffet. Drinks not included.

Hurlingham's
The New York Hilton/111 W.53rd St. (bet. 6th & 7th Aves.)/265-1600
$24.75 per person/3 sittings: 11:30, 1 and 10 p.m./all major cards
Another superspread with over 30 hot and cold dishes to choose from in an ultra-romantic setting. Includes one cocktail.

King Cole Room
St. Regis Hotel/2 E.55th St./872-6140/6161
$39.50/noon-3/all major
For a hefty price, a very hefty indulgence of seafood, hot dishes, salads galore, a carvery, roast duck and on and on, plus half a bottle of champagne each and Maxfield Parrish's adorable mural, too.

Mindy's
The Helmsley Hotel
212 E.42nd St. (bet. 1st & 2nd Aves.)/490-8900
$28.50/noon-3/all major
Endless champagne and endless trips to the buffet for lobster salad, shrimp, salmon, roasts, fresh omelettes, et al. All in Leona Helmsley's elegant and subdued pink and mirrored creation.

CHINESE RESTAURANTS

david yeadon ©

1 Auntie Yuan
1191 1st Ave. (off E.64th St.)/744-4040
Expensive/Daily noon-midnight/Amex
Sophisticated setting for innovative culinary combinations, (nouvelle chinoise) and striking arrangement of ingredients. Uneven but never boring.

2 Canton
45 Division St. (bet. E.Broadway & The Bowery)/226-4441
Moderate/T-Su noon-10/no cards
Exquisite Cantonese cuisine, especially fish and seafood dishes. A rediscovery of a much abused regional cuisine. If there's a crowd, a worthy alternative is **Siu Lam Kung** at 18 Elizabeth St., south of Canal, 732-0974.

3 Fu's
1395 2nd Ave. (bet. E.72nd & E.73rd St.)/517-9670
Expensive/Daily noon-midnight/all major
Great if you can get in for Gloria Chu's gourmet delights. A relative newcomer, but it's here to stay.

4 Hwa Yuan Szechuan Inn
40 East Broadway (bet. Catherine & Market Sts.)/966-5534
Moderate/Su-Th noon-10, F&S noon-11/all major
The nondescript decor disguises this minor mecca of authentic palate-popping Szechuan cookery.

5 Oriental Town Seafood
14 Elizabeth St. (South of Canal St.)/619-0085
Inexpensive/Daily 9 a.m. -11 p.m./no cards
Typical cramped Chinatown setting for a magnificent array of seafood creations, featuring fresh oysters, conch, the sweetest scallops imaginable and whole sea bass.

6 Phoenix Garden
The arcade between The Bowery and Elizabeth St./962-8934
Inexpensive/T-Su 11:30-10:30/no cards
The setting is forgettable, but the cuisine is consistently excellent Cantonese. Unusually good lemon chicken. Close eyes, open mouth.

7 Say Eng Look
5 East Broadway (off Chatham Square)/732-0796
Inexpensive/Daily 11:15-10:30 (F&S till 11:30)/Amex
Gastronomic treats à la Shanghai here (eel, shrimp seeds, sea cucumber) in newly renovated digs. Town's richest sauces.

8 Shun Lee Palace
155 E.55th St. (bet. Lexington & 3rd Aves.)/371-8844
Expensive/Daily noon-11, F&S till midnight/Amex, DC, CB
Touchstone of posh uptown in Chinese fare featuring unusual Hunan and Szechuan specialties. Sometimes too crowded. (Also try late night dim sum at **Shun Lee West**, 43 W.65th St./595-8895.)

9 Sichuan Pavilion
310 E.44th St. (bet. 1st & 2nd Aves.)/972-7377
Moderate/Daily noon-10/Amex
A welcome relief with California touches, a fresh selection of appetizers and a bevy of beautiful dishes for the adventurous.

0 Tse Yang
34 E.51st St./688-5447
Expensive/Daily noon-midnight/all major
Indulge in sumptuous, sybaritic settings on someone else's expense account, if you can. Wonderful, innovative and sinfully delicious.

FRENCH RESTAURANTS

1 Aurora

60 E.49th St. (bet. Madison & Park Aves.)/692-9292
Very expensive/M-F noon-2:30, 5:30-10:45, S 5:30-11/cl. Su/Amex,
CB, DC

Wonderfully imaginative French-inspired delicacies served in a spacious, exotic stage-setting created by none other than Milton Glaser. Joe Baum (**The Four Seasons** & **Windows on the World**) has succeeded again after a hesitant start.

2 Chantarelle

89 Grand St. (at Greene St.)/966-6960
Very expensive/T-S 6:30-10:30 cl. Su-M/Amex, MC, V

Cocooned in a block blessedly removed from the clatter of West Broadway, David and Karen Waltuck's highly-acclaimed eatery holds forth in muted elegance. Rely on the deferential, well-drilled staff to guide you through the excellent, limited-choice menus at the ten linen-draped tables.

La Côte Basque *see THE TOP TEN RESTAURANTS*

3 Lafayette

Drake Hotel/65 E.56th St./832-1565
Very Expensive/M-F noon-2:15, 6-9:30/all major

Breaking all our rules, we include this sophisticated new-comer in the belief that Chef Louis Outhier has created a superlative addition to the city's coterie of classical French restaurants. We watch with wonder!

4 La Grenouille

3 E.52nd St. (bet. 5th & Madison Aves.)/752-1495
Very expensive/T-S noon-2:30, 6-11:30/cl. Su-M/Amex, DC

Though it's taken some hits lately, we think there's still much to recommend here. The Gallic charm begins with the numerous floral arrangements spread about the dining room, as well as at the tables. Don't pass up the filet of sole or the exquisite billi-bi soup—a masterful marriage of mussels, seafood broth and cognac.

5 La Tulipe

104 W.13th St. (at 6th Ave.)/691-8860
Expensive/T-Su 6:30-10:30/cl. M/all major

Our nomination for the Village's best Français feed. It's small and warm, with a lovely burgundy-hued seating area blessedly uncongested and quiet.

Le Cirque *see THE TOP TEN RESTAURANTS*

6 Le Cygne

55 E.54th St./759-5941
Expensive/M-F noon-2, 6-10, S 6-11/cl. Su/all major

A festive spot, albeit expensive. As we've noted elsewhere, we can't resist scallops whenever they're offered, and this kitchen's presentation, starring a sensational saffron sauce, is now on our "must have again" list.

7 Le Perigord Park

575 Park Ave. (at E.63rd St.)/752-0050
Very expensive/T-F noon-2, 6-10:30, S 6-11/cl. Su-M/all major cards

The Park Ave. crowd (older, monied and more traditional types) are very loyal to this eatery—and this fact, for better or for worse, resonates in the menu and the ambience. While there are a few surprises, disappointments are equally rare, unless you're a dessert hound. (More gastronomic innovations may be found at the more intimate **Le Perigord** 405 E.52nd St. at 1st Ave.)

Lutèce *see THE TOP 10 RESTAURANTS*

GARDEN RESTAURANTS

1 American Festival Café
20 W.50th St. (at Rockefeller Center)/246-6699
Moderate/Daily noon-11, Su till 9/all major

While not top-flight from a culinary standpoint, the salads and simple preparations normally please and the outdoor dining overlooking the skating rink is always a joy. *(see THE SEA GRILL, in this listing)*

2 Barbetta
321 W.46th (bet. 8th & 9th Aves.)/246-9171
Moderate/M-S noon-11:30/Amex, DC, MC, V

A delightful stop in the theatre district, though matinee days can get a little frantic. They dispense an unsurprising but solid Italian menu. We are particularly taken with their home-made tortellini.

3 Giordano
409 W.39th St. (at 9th Ave.)/947-9811
Expensive/M-Th noon-11:30, F&S noon-midnight/all major

An out-of-the-way gem, right behind the up ramp to the Port Authority Bus Terminal! They practically kiss you on both cheeks as you walk in the door and their presence blesses an otherwise dreary block.

4 Lion's Rock
316 E.77th St. (bet. 1st & 2nd Aves.)/988-3610
Moderate/11:30-midnight/all major

A casual East Side bistro, popular with the spritzer and quiche crowd. The garden is best enjoyed during off-hours, when the elbowing throngs aren't present. The brunches are delightful, so try one in warm weather.

5 Provence
38 MacDougal St. (bet. Houston & Prince Sts.)/475-7500
Moderate/T-Su noon-11:30 p.m./Amex, DC, CB

Formerly Gordon's, a neighborhood favorite for northern Italian cuisine, this snug establishment is now in the hands of a Frenchman. His dishes, particularly those lamb, rabbit and veal creations are tantalizing samples of his homeland's southern region.

6 Ruc
312 E.72nd St. (bet. 1st & 2nd Aves.)/650-1611
Moderate/M-F 5-10:30 S & Su 12-10:30/all major

One of the last little Czech restaurants in this once Eastern European enclave. Wonderful roast goose, duck and pork, dumplings with red cabbage, goulash galore with paprika and romantic summer dining in the garden.

7 The Sea Grill
19 W.49th St./246-9201
Expensive/Daily, noon-3, 5-11, Su till 8:30/all major

As the garden is one-third of the Rockefeller Skating Rink (the American Festival Café, their gastronomic cousin, occupies the rest) they have arguably the most extraordinary al fresco dining in the city. Their simpler entrées are usually up to the location's sublime design.

8 Tavern on The Green
In Central Park at W.67th St./873-3200
Expensive/Daily 10-3:30, 5-1/all major

Location has always been their greatest asset, and the garden, especially in spring, is the loveliest, most bucolic of them all. The rapture comes more from dancing under the stars than the kitchen, although the food is fancily adequate.

ITALIAN RESTAURANTS

1 Cent' Anni
50 Carmine St. (off Bleecker St.)/989-9494
Expensive/M-F noon-2:20, 5:30-11, S 5:30-11:30, Su 5-11/Amex
A stalwart outpost for Florentine cooking, deceivingly modest in appearance and presentation. The seafood, and everything else, is always fresh. Lots of cheek-kissing here.

2 DeMarco
1422 3rd Ave. (bet. E.81st & E.82nd Sts.)/744-2819
Expensive/M-S 6-11/cl. Su/Amex, DC, CB
A sophisticated, ultra-cool establishment with stiletto spotlights on bouquets of flowers, soaring columns and not much else—slightly hi-tech, with hi-quality seafood, pure pastas and grilled veal in rich wine sauce, topped off with superb zabaglione.

3 Erminia
250 E.83rd St. (bet. 2nd & 3rd Aves.)/879-4284
Expensive/M-S 7 and 9/cl. Su/Amex
The latest from the Lattanzi family (the powers behind **Trastevere's** throne, 309 E.89th St./734-6343), a veritable dynasty of this genre. We like the intimacy here, and we adore Mama's angel hair pasta.

4 Felidia
243 E.58th St. (bet. 2nd & 3rd Aves.)/758-1479
Expensive/M-F 12-3, 5-12, S 5-12/cl. Su/all major cards
Some of the most succulent veal we've ever savored has been dished on these premises. We're particularly partial to the saltimbocca.

5 Il Mulino
86 W.3rd St. (bet. Thompson & Sullivan Sts.)/673-3783
Expensive/M-F noon-2:30, 5-11, S 5-11/cl. Su/Amex
Word has traveled about this homey bistro; now you have to wait for a table nearly every day at any hour. It's eminently worth it, however. Everything from the soup to the espresso and the not-over-extravagant bottom line is delightful. A bit noisy at peak time, though.

6 Il Nido
251 E.53rd St. (bet. 2nd & 3rd Aves.)/753-8450
Expensive/M-S noon-2:15, 5:30-10:15/cl. Su/all major cards
The offspring of **Il Monello** (1460 2nd Ave./535-9310) and a more sedate, formal environment than many of its brethren. Like its estimable parent, a superlative wine list is offered with justifiable pride. And try the carbonara—a definite diet-destroyer!

7 Parioli Romanissimo
24 E.81st St./288-2391
Very expensive/T-S 6-11/cl. Su & M/Amex, CB, DC
Formerly on 1st Avenue, this refined establishment seems to fit comfortably in its new brownstone home. No doubt the latest lease is somewhat responsible for the elevated prices. If you're celebrating, try the enormous rack of lamb (with bill to match). And don't miss their white truffles.

8 Primavera
1578 1st Ave. (at E.82nd St.)/861-8608
Expensive/Daily, 5:30-12/all major
One of the most pleasing eateries specializing in northern Italian traditions holds forth on the Upper East Side. The tortellini is terrific.

Rao *see UNUSUAL RESTAURANTS*

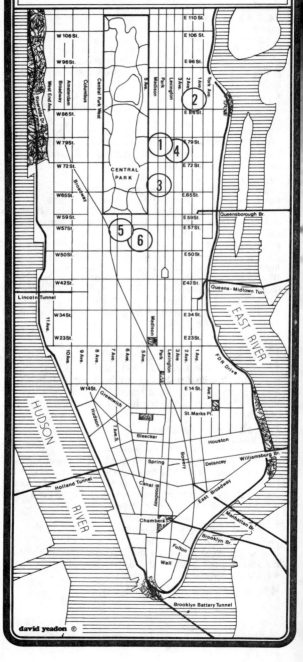

PEOPLE-WATCHING RESTAURANTS

1 Café Carlyle
Carlyle Hotel
35 E.76th (at Madison Ave.)/744-1600
Expensive/Breakfast 7-11, M-S noon-6, M-S 6-11, Su 7-11, Su brunch noon-6/all major

The high and the mighty have been haunting this palatial dining room since before and after John Kennedy designated it as the NY White House. Those of us who missed the 19th century applaud the revival of grand hotel rooms, and this one is certainly in the lead.

Christ Cella *see STEAK HOUSES*

2 Elaine's
1703 2nd Ave. (at E.88th St.)/534-8103
Expensive/M-F noon-2, S-Su 6-2/Amex only

One of a kind. This place proves our culture worships at the shrine of celebrity. Aside from its mystifying magnetism for showbiz and literary types and their hangers-ons, we don't really understand its appeal.

3 Le Cirque
58 E.65th St. (bet. Madison & Park Aves.)/794-9292
Very expensive/M-S noon-2:45, 6-10:30 cl. Su/Amex, CB, DC

You almost need a pedigree just to call this place for a reservation. Politicos, including the Unindicted Co-conspirator and the current First Couple dine here when they're in town. Despite top level power-shifts the quality endures. And why not? The food is surpassed only by the ministrations of the staff.

Lutèce *see TOP TEN RESTAURANTS*

4 Mortimer's
1057 Lexington Ave. (at E.75th St.)/517-6400
Expensive/M-F noon-3:30, S & Su noon-4:30, Su-M 6-midnight, T-F 6-2 a.m./all major cards

Glenn Bernbaum's 'in' club for the already 'in;' others will feel quite 'out' before they're even halfway in, and as the food is fashionably neutral, it's really an experience for only the most devoted people watchers.

The Regency Hotel Restaurant *see UNUSUAL RESTAURANTS*

5 Russian Tea Room
150 W.57th St. (bet. 6th & 7th Aves.)/265-0947*Expensive/Su-F 11:30-midnight, S 11-midnight/all major*

Another favorite for the movers and shakers of the entertainment world. (That hysterically funny scene in "Tootsie" wasn't arbitrarily shot here.) There is good reason—the 3-martini lunch is very much alive and flourishes amongst the captains of midtown industry who inhabit its plush booths. Nureyev and the stars of music and dance nibble a little more judiciously in their niches.

6 21 Club
21 W.52nd St./582-7200
Expensive/daily noon-midnight, cl. weekends from July 4-Labor Day/Amex, DC, CB, MC and House Charge

One of the originals in this stuffiest of categories. Indeed, it began as a speakeasy (the quintessential discriminator) during Prohibition. Although it's not a private membership club, it acts as if it were and the precise pecking order proves it. The aura of New York's glory days is still intoxicatingly apparent here despite the recent facelift and menu changes.

ROMANTIC RESTAURANTS

david yeadon ©

Note: While beauty and romantic ambience are crucial here, we still insist on a high standard of delectables, whatever the price.

1 Café des Artistes
1 W.67th St. (at Central Park West)/877-3500
Moderate/M-S 5:30-12:30, Su 5-11/all major
An interesting menu featuring excellent duck confit, spicy steak tartare and simply garnished seafood in a room adorned with frolicking nude nymphs, the inspired work of Howard Chandler Christy. Wonderful.

2 Café Nicholson
333 E.58th St. (bet. 1st and 2nd Aves.)/355-6789
Expensive/call for details
Marvelous! A restaurateur who caters only to clients when the creative urge surges in a setting of ultimate romance.

La Grenouille *see FRENCH RESTAURANTS*

3 Maxim's
680 Madison Ave. (bet. E.61st & E.62nd St.s)/751-5111
Very expensive/6-1, cl. Su/all major
An extravagant experience in this exotic art nouveau re-creation, but worth it for an ultra-romantic night on the town, dressed to the nines. (And the food's not bad either!)

4 One if By Land, Two if By Sea
17 Barrow St. (bet. W.4th & 7th Ave.)/255-8649
Expensive/Daily 6-midnight/all major
A hidden delight in Aaron Burr's old carriage house with just about every romantic nuance—fireplace, candles, cocktail piano and superb Beef Wellington!

5 Petrossian
182 W.58th St. (at 7th Ave.)/245-2214
Very expensive/M-S 11-1, cl. Su/all major
When only the best will suffice—caviar in all colors, truffles, foie gras and bubbly all night long in a sumptuous brass and glass setting. "Taste teasers," too, for the timid of purse.

6 River Café
1 Water St./Cadman Plaza, Brooklyn at East River, under the Brooklyn Bridge/718-522-5200
Very expensive/Daily noon-2:30, 6:30-11/all major
Admittedly, we find chef-manager Charles Palmer's creations sometimes overblown and invariably over-priced, but—ah! The waterfront vistas of the city and the ambience of utter indulgence justify inclusion.

7 Sign of the Dove
1110 3rd Ave. (at E.65th St.)/861-8080
Expensive/Daily 6-11/all major
Ever-so-pretty and sophisticated with recent major reformations to counteract the critics. Give it another chance, New Yorkers.

Tavern on the Green *see GARDEN RESTAURANTS*

The Terrace *see UNUSUAL RESTAURANTS*

The Water Club *see SIDEWALK CAFES*

Windows on the World *see TOURIST ATTRACTIONS*

8 The World Yacht Club
Pier 62 at the foot of W.23rd St./929-7090
Expensive/7-10 nightly/all major
If food is not of primary importance, here's a delightful way to spend an evening dining and dancing à deux and sailing the harbor in one of four "Restaurant Yachts;" an unforgettable dining & dancing experience.

SEAFOOD RESTAURANTS

david yeadon ©

Gage & Tollner
372 Fulton St. (bet. Pearl & Jay Sts.)/718-875-5181
Moderate/M-F noon-9:30, S 4-10:30/all major
(We've squeezed in our Brooklyn favorite!) An experience in antiquity—a lovely old mahogany/mirrored restaurant which offers fascinating forgotten dishes and basic broilings and poachings. Well worth the trip.

1 Gloucester House
37 E.50th St./755-7394
Expensive/M-F noon-2:30, 5:30-10, S & Su noon-10/jacket & tie/all major
Outstanding appetizers, seafood and in-season fish (even finnan haddie and smelt). Snooty service in the masculine upmarket, nautical decor and matching prices.

2 Jane Street Seafood Café
31 8th Ave. (at Jane St.)/243-9237
Inexpensive/Su-Th 5:30-11, F & S till midnight/Amex, MC, V
New England touches in this friendly informal space known for the freshest seafood and exceptional steamed mussels, flounder and wonderful bluefish.

3 John Clancy's
181 W.10th St. (at 7th Ave. So)/242-8350
Very expensive/M-S 6-11:30, Su 5-10:30/all major
Lovely village basement niche featuring superb mesquite-grilled fish and excellent desserts. Full of adoring admirers.

4 Le Bernardin
155 W.51st St. (bet. 6th & 7th Aves.)/489-1515
Very expensive/M-S noon-2:15, 6-10:30/cl. Su/all major cards
A relative newcomer, Gilbert Le Coze has already established a reputation for spectacularly fresh and simply served seafood in a sophisticated and sublime setting. An experience to treasure.

5 Marylou's
21 W.9th St. (off 5th Ave.)/533-0012
Moderate/M-F 11:30-3:00, 5:30-1, F&S till 2, Su noon-4, 5:30-10:45/all major
Fine townhouse setting, friendly staff, frisky (and famous) crowd, the freshest of fish, a mesquite grill and praiseworthy desserts (even the rice pudding!).

6 Oyster Bar & Restaurant
Grand Central Terminal (lower level)/490-6050
Moderate/M-F 11:30-9:30/all major
Forget the tiled/crypt-like decor, the din and the rush and enjoy a vast array of the best fish dishes in town with superlative clam chowders, oysters and an exemplary wine list.

7 Pesca
25 E.22nd St. (off Broadway)/533-2293
Moderate/M-F 12-3, S 6-midnight, Su 6-10/all major
Pleasantly informal place offering a vast choice of dishes with Italian overtones (great cioppino).

The Sea Grill *see GARDEN RESTAURANTS*

8 Wilkinson's Café
1573 York Ave. (at E.83rd St.)/535-5454
Expensive/Daily 6-11/Amex, DC
Delightful upmarket, uptown corner; an intimate setting for innovative seafood creations and terrific chocolate cake for dessert.

STEAK HOUSES

Christ Cella
160 E.46th St. (bet. 3rd & Lexington Aves.)/697-2497
Expensive/M-S noon-10:30/all major
No frills, no menu, no open necks, please. And no rude remarks about the supercilious staff. But definitely a yes for the top-flight beef and seafood.

Frank's
431 W.14th St. (bet. 9th & 10th Aves.)/243-1349
Moderate/M-T 4-a.m. 3 p.m., 5-10 p.m., F & S 5-11/all major
Basic meat market establishment (they add tablecloths for dinner) with wonderful steaks and the famed Molinari home-style cuisine. Ask about the nightly mushroom specials.

Gage & Tollner *see SEAFOOD RESTAURANTS*

Gallagher's
228 W.52nd St. (off Broadway)/245-5336
Moderate/Daily noon-midnight/all major
A true bastion of New York masculinity—a former speakeasy, now a serious steak house reeking with power, politics, insider trader and sportstalk traditions.

Palm
837 2nd Ave. (bet. E.44th & E.45th Sts.)/687-2953
Expensive/M-F noon-11:30, S 5-11:30/all major
The touchstone of NY steakhouses. . .cramped, clubby, saw-dusty, menuless, unservile service, vast platters of the best steaks, chops, lobsters, onion rings, and homemade potato chips. **Palm Too** across the street is for the overspill.

Peter Luger
178 Broadway (Driggs Ave. near The Williamsburg Bridge)/718-387-7400/Brooklyn
Expensive/Daily noon-3 and then 5:45-9:45, F&S till 10:45/no cards/
A rare non-Manhattan institution. Splendidly staid place for steaklovers who crave excellent desserts as well. Worth the effort.

Pietro's
232 E.43rd St. (bet. 2nd & 3rd Aves.)/682-9760
Expensive/M-F noon-2:30, 5:30-10:30, S 5:30-10:30, cl. Su June-October/Amex
In spite of a large Italian array of veal, chicken and seafood dishes, the steaks here are the main attraction, with generous-spirited portions for a gregarious and occasionally gluttonous clientele.

Smith & Wollensky
201 E.49th St. (at 3rd Ave.)/753-1530
Expensive/M-F noon-11:30, S&Su 5-11:30/all major
Some find this "old town" place a little too popular and self-conscious, encouraging expense account excesses. We enjoy its dependability, generosity and affable character—plus, unlike **Palm**, there's room to move around.

Sparks
210 E.46th St. (bet. 2nd & 3rd Aves.)/687-4855
Expensive/M-S noon-3, 5-11/all major
Uneven, but still one of the tops if you stick to the steaks exclusively and find pleasure in an informed wine list. Not as generous as some of the others, though.

Wally's & Joseph's
249 W.49th St. (bet. 8th Ave. & Broadway)/582-0460
Expensive/M-F noon-3, 4:40-11:30, S 4:30-11:30/all major
Ideal pre-post theatre splurge with enormous steaks, generous side dishes (unusually good pasta) and a pleasant pubby atmosphere.

24-HOUR EATERIES

david yeadon ©

1 Around the Clock Café
E.9th St. & 3rd Ave./598-0402
Inexpensive/no cards
A relative newcomer to the St. Mark's scene and always packed after midnight. Coffee shop decor, but the real color comes from the East Village clients.

2 Astor Riviera Café
454 Astor Pl. (at Lafayette St.)/677-4461
Moderate/all major
A familiar kind of place, friendly and filled with students and residents from SoHo, NoHo and the East Village. Happy and harmless.

3 The Brasserie
100 E.53rd St. (bet. Lexington & Park Aves.)/751-4840
Moderate/all major
This casual grill boasts that it never closes, even during blackouts. They will cook anything to order as long as they have the ingredients. Friendly, too.

4 Chinatown
A useful resource: **Hong Fat** and a number of other basic share-a-table places along Mott and adjoining streets stay open until at least 5 a.m., and sometimes 24 hours. Bok choy and black bean sauce for breakfast, anyone?

5 Empire Diner
210 10th Ave. (at W.22nd St.)/243-2736
Moderate/Amex
We admit to late-night forays into Northern New Jersey, the national capital of diners, so we are biased toward such establishments. An art deco gem that lights up Chelsea nights like a beacon, dishing out honest, hearty fare. Sidewalk tables in summer.

6 Kiev International
117 2nd Ave. (at E.7th St.)/674-4040
Inexpensive/no cards
What a whopping spread of Eastern European goodies—pirogi, blintzes, stuffed cabbage and wonderful soups. Nothing fancy, you understand—just honest and wholesome.

7 Lox Around the Clock
676 6th Ave. (at W.21st St.)/691-3535
Moderate/all major
An amusing if erratic late-night diversion featuring Borscht-belt cuisine with bar and a Munster-like dining area off to one side for more private types.

8 The Market Diner
11th Ave (at W.43rd St.)/244-6033
256 West St. (off Laight St.)/925-0856
Inexpensive/no cards
There are only two left. The one on 43rd & 11th is an experience. Ask UPS truck drivers, hookers, pimps and other steady clientele. But the food at both is good, generous and served with gusto. The one downtown is the home of civil servants.

9 103 Second Ave.
2nd Ave. & E.6th St./533-0769
Moderate/no cards
It always feels a little like New Year's Eve here, even during the summer months; a wonderfully loud jukebox filled with solid gold; spicy chili and generous breakfast specials.

UNUSUAL RESTAURANTS

Map labels:

W 106 St.
W 96 St.
W 86 St.
W 79 St.
W 72 St.
W 65 St.
W 59 St.
W 57 St.
W 50 St.
W 42 St.
W 34 St.
W 23 St.
W 14 St.

E 110 St.
E 106 St.
E 96 St.
E 86 St.
E 79 St.
E 72 St.
E 65 St.
E 59 St.
E 57 St.
E 50 St.
E 42 St.
E 34 St.
E 23 St.
E 14 St.

West End Ave.
Riverside Dr.
Amsterdam
Broadway
Columbus
Central Park West
5 Am.
Madison
Park
Lexington
3 Ave.
2 Ave.
1 Ave.
York Ave.
Ave. A

CENTRAL PARK

Broadway

11 Ave.
10 Ave.
9 Ave.
8 Ave.
7 Ave.
6 Ave.
5 Ave.
Park
Madison
Lexington
3 Ave.
2 Ave.
1 Ave.

HUDSON RIVER
EAST RIVER
F D R Drive

Lincoln Tunnel
Queens - Midtown Tun.
Queensborough Br.

Greenwich
Hudson
7 Ave. S.
Bleecker
St. Marks Pl.
Houston
Spring
Bowery
Delancey
Williamsburg Br.
Holland Tunnel
Canal
Broadway
East Broadway
Chambers
Manhattan Br.
Brooklyn Br.
Fulton
Wall
Brooklyn Battery Tunnel

david yeadon ©

1 Cabana Carioca
123 W.45th St. (bet. 7th & 8th Aves.)/581-8088
Moderate/M-Th noon-11, F till 1, S 4-1/cl. Su/all major
Frenzied Brazil-in-carnival atmosphere, everyone talking and
moving at breakneck speed. It must be the kick in those
enormous spicy platters.

2 Cellar in the Sky
1 World Trade Center (107th floor)/938-1111
$75 + /call for details/all major
Exotic **Windows on the World** setting for a marvelous marathon 7-course dinner experience with wines to match each
course. Reservations essential.

3 Chez Louis *1016 2nd Ave. (bet. E.53rd & E.54th*
Sts.)/752-1400
Expensive/M-F 12-3, 6-midnight, S 6-midnight, Su 5-10/all major
David Liederman of David's Cookies fame and wife Susan
have got it right once again with their bounteous French
bistro—serving enormous platters of everything. Farewell
nouvelle!

4 El Internacional
219 W.Broadway (near White St.)/226-8131
Moderate/11:30-1/all major
Sample the tapas bar at least once, it's the second best in
town. **(The Ballroom** on 253 W.28th St/244-3005 is tops.)
Then take the time to watch the weirdest crowds in an even
weirder setting.

Frank's *see STEAK HOUSES*
Great Jones St. Café *see VALUE RESTAURANTS*

5 Gulf Coast and The Aquacade
489 W.12th St. (at West St.)/206-8790
Inexpensive/M-Th 5-11:45, F & S till 1, Su 4-11:30/no cards
A candidate for the best Louisiana homestyle cooking this
side of the Mason-Dixon line, the best blue margaritas and
steamed shrimp at unbeatable prices. Crowded, cozy & crazy.

Rao's
455 E.144th St. (at Pleasant Ave.)/534-9625
Moderate/M-F 6-11, cl. S & Su/no cards
This place has only six tables and it can take months to get
in. When you do, they offer waist-swelling, loaded Italian
dishes with stupendous seafood salad appetizer.

6 Regency Hotel Restaurant
540 Park Ave. (at E.61st St.)/759-4100
Expensive/Breakfast 7-11 a.m./all major
Home of the new(ish) NYork tradition—the BIG power breakfast of champions—for powerbrokers par excellence. Fascinating the first time.

Silverbird *see UNUSUAL NIGHTS SPOTS*
Sylvia's
328 Lenox Ave. (at W.127th St.)/534-9414
Moderate/M-S 7:30 a.m. 10 p.m./Su brunch with music/no cards
Known in Harlem as the undisputed "Queen of Soul Food."
We're hardly experts, but the spare ribs are definitely the best
we've tasted. Also try the huge daily breakfasts from 7:30-10
a.m.

The Terrace
Butler Hall/Columbia University
400 W.119th St. (bet. Amsterdam and Morningside Dr.)/666-9490
Expensive/T-F noon-2:30, T-S 6-10/all major
This romantic rooftop refuge offers fantastic city vistas and
top-flight French cuisine in a truly unexpected location.

VALUE RESTAURANTS

Note: All of the following offer unusually good values in terms of quality cuisine and service; in most instances the average price of a 3-course dinner before drinks and tips is less than $20 per person.

1 Abyssinia
35 Grand St. (at Thompson St.)/226-5959
Authentic lip-smacking, hand-eaten (optional) African dishes.

2 Anar Bagh
338 E.6th St. (bet. 1st & 2nd Aves.)
One of the best along this redolent street of inexpensive Indian and Pakistani restaurants. Also check out the nearby **Passage to India**.

3 Benito's
174½ Mulberry St. (bet. Grand & Broome Sts.)/226-9171
Basic, brash, boisterous, and very Sicilian, this place is always popular.

4 Billy's
948 1st Ave. (bet. E.52nd & E.53rd St.)/355-8920
Salt-of-the-earth neighborhood nook and excellent value for steaks, chops and chummy atmosphere.

5 Cabana Carioca
123 W.45th St. (bet. 6th & 7th Aves.)/581-8088
Enormous spicy platters of inexpensive Brazilian cuisine. Great!

6 Cucina Staglione
275 Bleecker St. (bet. 6th & 7th Aves.)/924-2707
Most popular budget Italian restaurant in the Village and deservedly so.

7 El Faro
823 Greenwich St. (at Horatio St.)/929-8210
The best of at least seven similar places in the area offering more than generous Spanish seafood and chicken dishes.

8 Great Jones St. Café
54 Great Jones St. (at The Bowery)/675-9304
Tiny, cramped, terrible decor and fantastic Cajun dishes.

9 Gulf Coast and the Aquacade
489 W.12th St. (at West St.)/206-8790
Louisiana-Cajun cooking at its best with atmosphere and margaritas to match—plus those steamed shrimp and crayfish!!!

10 Mocca Hungarian
1588 2nd Ave. (bet. E.82nd St. & E.83rd St.)/734-6470
All waist-wasting Eastern European delights at superbudget prices.

11 Odessa
117 Ave. A (bet. E.7th & E.8th Sts.)/473-8916
Ditto for delectable Ukrainian delicacies.

12 Sabor
20 Cornelia St. (bet. W.4th & Bleecker Sts.)/243-9579
Button-busting Cuban cuisine and marvelous margaritas.

13 Tandoor
40 E.49th St. (bet. Park & Madison Aves.)/752-3334
$10 lunchtime Indian buffet extravaganza with Tandoori treats.

14 Veselka Coffee Shop
144 2nd Ave. (bet. E.9th & St. Marks Pl.)/228-9682
Surprising range of Eastern European dishes in coffee shop setting and neighborhood center. (Bring a book, even.)

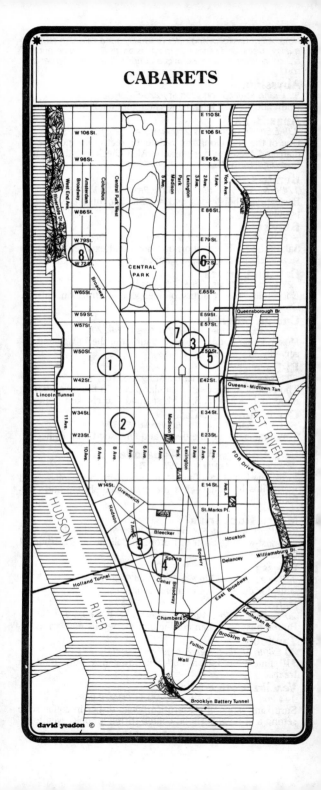

CABARETS

1 Backstage/Square Meals
315 W.45th St. (bet. 8th & 9th Aves.)/489-6100
Moderate/$10 cov./all major
Sophisticated, funny and star-studded cabaret in the back room of this very pretty pre-post-theatre eatery with Oriental overtones.

2 The Ballroom
253 W.28th St. (bet. 7th & 8th Aves.)/244-3005
Moderate/all major
In addition to being the best tapas bar in the city, the cabaret acts vary and are top-notch. This pioneer also serves as an art gallery featuring Blossom Dearie and more.

Bill's Gay Nineties *see UNUSUAL NIGHTSPOTS*

Café Carlyle *see PIANO ROOMS*

3 Café Versailles *see DINING & DANCING*
151 E.50th St. (bet. 3rd & Lexington Aves.)/753-3429
Expensive/all major
Folies Bergere showgirls with bolla spinners, singers and ballet duos sometimes, as well as magicians. The belly dancers are upstairs at **Club Ibis**.

Chippendale's *see UNUSUAL NIGHTSPOTS*

5 & 10, No Exaggeration *see UNUSUAL NIGHTSPOTS*

4 Greene Street Café
101 Greene St. (bet. Spring & Prince Sts.)/925-2415
Moderate/$12.50 cov. $10 min., can vary/all major
A reputation as a steamy SoHo spot for all sorts of things, from cabaret to jazz to food to wine. Terrific jungle decor in an ex-bare-brick garage with all the trimmings.

5 Freddy's Supper Club
308 E.49th St. (bet. 1st & 2nd Aves.)/888-1633
Expensive/call ahead for cov./Amex
Frothy, fun and upcoming talents, including the charms of Fran Jeffries and good jazz while dining on better than decent food. They audition regularly for newcomers.

Michael's Pub *see JAZZ CLUBS*

6 Mr. Sam's
1265 3rd Ave. (bet. E.72nd and E.73rd Sts.)/517-2020
Moderate/$10 cov./they ask you to call ahead/all major, except DC
Posh and elegant supper club hosted by Valentine, who sings. Good chanteuses, colorful cabarets and urbane attitudes make for pleasant diversions. It's romantic, too!.

7 Monkey Bar
Elysée Hotel/60 E.54th St. (bet. Madison & Park Aves.)/753-1066/
Moderate/$12 min. for show/all major
One of the original comedy cabarets and still a favorite with the well-heeled crowd.

8 Palsson's
158 W.72nd St. (off Broadway)/595-7400
Moderate/$6 cov., $6 min./Amex, MC M
The upstairs cabaret is a satirical take-off on current and classic Broadway hits, with a twist of irony and a gaggle of giggles. Off the midtown beaten track; worth the trip.

9 S.O.B. (Sounds of Brazil)
204 Varick St. (at W.Houston St.)/243-4940
Expensive/call for various covers/all major
Exubert high ceilinged multi-purpose, samba'ed, salsa'ed salon with carnival spirit that's super sassy and sizzling with heavy Latin accents.

COMEDY CLUBS

david yeadon ©

1 Caroline's
332 8th Ave (bet. W.26th & W.27th Sts.)/924-3499
Pier 17 at The South Street Seaport/924-3499
Inexpensive/cov. varies/Amex, MC, V
One of the funnier of the funny clubs with 90-minute shows
nightly. HBO kind of homey, and with even more room in the
Seaport digs.

2 Catch a Rising Star
1487 1st Ave. (off E.77th St.)/794-1906
Inexpensive/cov. $7-10/Amex
A New York original, always good for a solid laugh, rarely
misses the mark and a pioneer for new comics who eventually
make it on both coasts and the vidscreens.

3 Comedy U
55 Grand St. (off W. Broadway)/431-4022
Cov. varies, dinner included for $35/Call first/no cards
A worthwhile stand-up experience, in an area that's easily
accessible without the phoney stuff the bigger clubs hand out.
This place also offers classes, and was established by people
serious about laughter.

4 Dangerfield's
1118 1st Ave. (bet. E.61st & E.62nd Sts.)/593-1650
Moderate/Cover never higher than $15/all major
Borscht Belt comedy dished out by the director of dramatic
comedy and his denizens of the night. Usually funny, always
packed, and you'll never know who you'll find standing up
front.

5 Downstairs at Who's on First
1205 1st Av. (at E.61st St.)/737-2772
Moderate/Call first/Amex
They have a women's comedy night here, they allow auditions
and they're very funny, too, without prohibitive prices. Peter
Spellos is the man in charge of this teeny basement hideaway
that's worth seeking out.

6 The Duplex
55 Grove St. (off 7th Ave. So.)/255-5438
Moderate/cov. varies/no cards
The institution that launched Joan Rivers, Woody Allen
and a whole slew of top-notchers who graduated to TV is still
going strong on a busy Village corner. Pop in.

7 Goodtimes
449 3rd Ave. (at E.31st St.)/686-4250
Moderate/cov.varies/all major
Generous food, generous laughs, daily concerts, auditions
and the more the merrier. It's almost a marathon of nonstop
giggles when it gets going.

8 The Improvisation
358 W.44th St. (at 9th Ave.)/765-8268
Inexpensive/cov. varies/no cards
This is the original one, which gets knocked off every night
on the boob-tube and out on the West Coast. Hard to top for
talent, fast laughs and political satire, sight gags and bad magicians.

9 Mostly Magic
55 Carmine St. (at Bedford St.)/924-1472
Moderate/cov. varies/all major
A magical variety club that offers Sunday children's shows as
well as evening adult entertainments. It's the only magic
showcase in town, and only the best are allowed.

DINING & DANCING

david yeadon ©

1 Café Pierre
Pierre Hotel/2 E.61st St. (between 5th & Madison Aves.)/838-8000
Expensive/all major
All very elegant and proper and pleasantly old-fashioned trio music for delicate dancers. Just what you'd expect in this rather exclusive hotel.

2 Café Versailles
151 E.50th St. (bet. 3rd & Lexington Aves.)/753-3429
Expensive/all major
Continental menu with a decently sized ballroom-style dance floor, stage, cabaret and faintly Parisian tone. For a complete change of scene, try **Club Ibis** upstairs for belly dancing galore.

3 The Edwardian Room
The Plaza Hotel/59th St. and 5th Ave./759-3000
Moderate/all major
The hochest of a hochdeutsch Victorian dining room with romantic trappings for old-fashioned European dancing & dining in the grande dame of NY hotels.

4 Jimmy Weston's
131 E.54th St. (bet. Park & Lexington Aves.)/838-8384
Expensive/cov. varies/all major
The last of the high-society supper clubs in the grand tradition. Alternating trios nightly for dining & dancing in style.

5 Marriot Marquis
1700 Broadway at Times Square/398-1900
Moderate/all major
Dine in **The View** restaurant and dance in the revolving lounge to a live band—high hedonism here.

6 Maxim's
680 Madison Ave. (bet. E.61st & E.62nd Sts.)/751-5111
Very expensive/Amex
Dine and dance in Parisian elegance, pampered in a pure art nouveau setting with a Pierre Cardin/Escoffier style unparalleled on any avenue. Rich for the blood and very heady indeed.

7 Roma Di Notte
137 E.55th St. (off Lexington Ave.)/832-1128
Expensive/call first/all major
The name says it all: romantic, olive-skinned singers and strolling musicians, Roman statuary, marble dance floor and a mood of sweet abandon.

8 Roseland
239 W.52nd St. (at 7th Ave.)/247-0200
Moderate/call for details/no cards
She's back. Revamped and rejuvenated for traditional ballroom dancing wth snack buffet—no formal dining—plus disco on weekends. Unique and unsurpassed in its own way.

Stringfellow's *see DISCOS*

Tavern on the Green *see GARDEN RESTAURANTS*

9 37th St. Hideaway
32 W.37th St. (bet. 5th & 6th Aves.)/947-8940
Expensive/all major
Romantic dining and dancing to Rossano Brazzi types at the piano. While the food is not the best, the ambience certainly is, for swooning and swinging between courses and after dessert.

World Yacht *see ROMANTIC RESTAURANTS*

DISCOS

1 Area
157 Hudson St. (So. of Canal St.)/226-8423/$15-18/Amex only
Still known for its chameleon effects, this is one of the sole survivors of the pioneering days. (Studio 54 has died.) Mixed crowd, cooks after 11 p.m.; be prepared for everything, from punkettes to preppies.

2 4D
605 W.55th St. (off West Side Highway)/247-0628/$15-20/all
An outerspace planet, a cave and much more for the ardent dance crowd that doesn't quit. Live and luscious acts on stage, too, in discreet vogue. Not bad for singles either.

3 Heartbreak
179 Varick St. (off Carlton St.)/691-2388/$10-15/no cards
'50s & '60s fans must come here to this diner that transforms into a back-to-the-future scene. A TriBeCa tradition by now.

4 Kingfisher Room
67 Bleecker St./(off Broadway)/529-1147/$5 cov./no cards
This is the best of all the "yuppie" disco hangouts. The interior is draped in Persian drama, the service is civilized (as opposed to all the other yuppie discos), the music mix is good. Go for it.

Limelight *see SINGLES SPOTS*

5 Madame Rosa's
St John's Lane (off Beach, one block south of Canal, via Varick)/ 219-2207/$5 cov./no cards
Lounge and disco for the '90s with avant-garde, star-studded clientele, well-hidden with cachet and full of magic from the occult to the music mix.

6 Palladium
126 E.14th St. (off Irving Pl.)/473-7171/$6-20/Amex, MC, V
The direct descendant of Studio 54, but much, much bigger and better, with swirling banks of spots, wild-looking crowds after midnight, and all the verve and vibration of New York nightlife at the clubs. Never before 11 p.m. for the initiated.

7 Stringfellow's
35 E.21st St. (bet. Park Ave. So. & Madison Ave.)/254-2444/$25/all
Considered by the plastic snob set to be the best disco-restaurant in town for who it keeps out as well as who it lets in. Top-notch columnists wearing polyester have been banned, as have the fat cats who are really fat. For the chicly elegant only.

8 1018
W.18th St. and 10th Ave./645-5157/$10-18/no cards
This is for serious disco workouts and dancers (and the old Area crowd). The 5000-square-foot dance floor, the comfortable bar rails, the banquettes, the steamy music, the steamier crowd say it all. Brand new and becoming news. Earthy bunch from Brooklyn and the Bronx and all points between wear their colors to strut and stroll the perimeter, then they go out there and do it!

9 Tunnel
220 12th Ave. (entrance on W.27th St.)/244-6444/$10-20/no cards
The newest, most unique of spaces for drinking and dancing. Chelsea Mini Storage,a.k.a. The Terminal Warehouse,is now a 630 x 35-foot long train tunnel for followers of the latest fashion fads and lifestyles. New Wave, progressive and more.

HAPPY HOURS

david yeadon ©

1 Adam's Apple
1117 1st Ave. (at E.61st St.)/371-8651
Splendid buffet in this Garden of Eden disco, where it all began way back in the great days of the 1st Ave. singles strip.

2 Café Luxembourg
200 W.70th St. (bet. Broadway & West End Ave.)/873-7411
Chic-to-Chic crowd among the white tile/art deco highlights and definitive French-style happy hour selections which feature sliced spicy things, cheeses and crudités. Très gentil.

3 Cattleman
5 E.45th St./661-1200
A bit of the old western saloon atmosphere here with big steaks and whoop-it-up dancehall entertainment which begins after the famous happy hour delectables have disappeared.

4 Cavanaugh's
1450 Broadway (at W.41st St.)/719-4633
Handsomely woody and pleasantly tranquil until the office crowd roars in at 5 for the generous hot and cold buffet served up by the chef-carver of roast beef, ham and turkey.

5 Charlie Brown's
The Pan Am Building (off Vanderbilt and E.42nd St.)/661-2520
Paneled, pubby haven packed with the executive elite who pretend they're here for business, but have really come to down a few along with the well-filled plates from the generous buffet before hitting the domestic doldrums.

6 The Guv'nor
303 Madison Ave. (bet. E.41st & E.42nd Sts.)/867-0540
A perfect pausing place just by Grand Central Terminal, with pub-like atmosphere and a vast array of steam tables to choose from. They're a little heavy on the deep-fried stuff, but if your metabolism can take it, indulge.

7 Maude's
569 Lexington Ave. (The Summit Hotel at E.50th St.)/753-1515
All very Victorian, San Francisco style, and seemingly a franchise forerunner in flavor. Happy hour is packed with the singles crowd choosing from a healthy smorgasbord selection.

8 Molly Mog's
65 W.55th St. (off 6th Ave.)/581-5436
Where would the Rockefeller rogues and roguettes be without Molly and her awesome array of cold cuts, salads, pastas and occasional hot dishes? This relocated classic caters to those burned-out from political power-pandering at the office.

9 Nemo's Pub
1 E.48th St./736-0210
An almost convincing combo of Nautilus and Yellow Submarine with a piano and a respectable happy hour selection usually featuring roast beef as the mainstay, in a part of town not known for giveaways.

0 Reidy's
22 E.54th St./753-9419
Notable midtown watering-hole cocooned in a glass tower with power-play street-level bar and boisterous upstairs happy hot 'n'cold spread. Solid, just like Bill Reidy himself.

JAZZ CLUBS

david yeadon ©

1 Angry Squire
216 7th Ave. (bet. W.22nd & W.23rd Sts.)/242-9066
Moderate/Amex, MC, V
Landmark jazz showcased for serious listening with musical traditions that go way back to the beginnings of the era.

2 The Blue Note
131 W.3rd St. (off 6th Ave.)/475-8592
Moderate/cov. varies/Amex, MC, V
The fine shrine of jazz in New York, the key location, the place to be at. The best and the brightest do weekly shows here.

3 Bradley's
70 University Pl. (at E.10th St.)/228-6440
Moderate/$5 cov. & $5 min/Amex, DC
Dignified village fringe institution for supreme jazz, piano/ bass duo and top flight impromptu performances.

4 Carlos I
432 6th Ave. (off W.10th St.)/982-3260
Moderate/cov. varies/Amex, MC, V
A Village jazz institution with a reputation as a decent sea-food restaurant as well. Very popular with everyone—all classes, all colors, all jazz lovers.

5 Fat Tuesday's
190 3rd Ave. (at E.17th St.)/533-7902
Moderate/all major
First rate sessions beneath **Tuesday's** bar-restaurant—ideal for budding jazz fans and old cognoscenti.

6 Gregory's
1149 1st Ave. (at E.63rd St.)/371-2220
Inexpensive/all major
A tiny little jazz music box on the Upper East Side, where such things are scarce. Sorrow Aster is a sultry songstress who plays hostess to the jazz greats when they visit.

7 Michael's Pub
211 E.55th St. (bet. 2nd & 3rd Aves.)/758-2272
Expensive/cov. varies/all major
This is where Woody Allen plays his clarinet and where jazz cooks and chills. Call ahead, and don't let them toss you after the set. Celebs love it, too, so behave here, in a supper club setting that works well.

8 Sweet Basil
88 7th Ave. So. (at Bleecker St.)/242-1785
Moderate/Cov. varies/all major
A mellow mecca of mainstream jazz featuring the legendary trumpet of Doc Cheatham and others. Cozy, romantic and more, especially for the aficionados.

9 Sweetwater's
170 Amsterdam Ave. (at. W.68th St.)/873-4100
Moderate/Cov. varies/all major
Flashy, jazzy pop and rhythm 'n' blues in the best tradition, keeping cosmopolitan flavor mixed with funky from Harlem and cool from the Village.

0 Zinno
126 W.13th St. (bet. 6th & 7th Aves.)/924-5182
Moderate/all major
A refined spot for excellent chamber jazz and above-average cuisine on a street dotted with unusual trysting spots.

LITERARY WATERING HOLES

E 110 St.
E 106 St.
E 96 St.
W 106 St.
W 96 St.
West End Ave.
Broadway
Amsterdam
Columbus
Central Park West
W 86 St.
W 79 St.
W 72 St.
W 65 St.
W 59 St.
W 57 St.
W 50 St.
W 42 St.
W 34 St.
W 23 St.
Lincoln Tunnel
11 Ave.
10 Ave.
9 Ave.
8 Ave.
7 Ave.
6 Ave.
5 Ave.
Madison
Park
Lexington
W 14 St.
Greenwich
Bleecker
Bowery
Houston
Spring
Canal
Broadway
Holland Tunnel
Chambers
Fulton
Wall
HUDSON RIVER

CENTRAL PARK
5 Ave.
Madison
Park
Lexington
3 Ave.
2 Ave.
1 Ave.
York Ave.
E 86 St.
E 79 St.
E 72 St.
E 65 St.
E 59 St.
E 57 St.
E 50 St.
E 42 St.
E 34 St.
E 23 St.
E 14 St.
Ave. A
St. Marks Pl.
Delancey
East Broadway
Broadway

Queensborough Br.
Queens - Midtown Tun.
EAST RIVER
FDR Drive
Williamsburg Br.
Manhattan Br.
Brooklyn Br.
Brooklyn Battery Tunnel

david yeadon ©

1 The Algonquin Hotel
59 W.44th St./840-6800

Still popular with the literary set, the Rose Room's Round Table was famous for **THE NEW YORKER**'s glittering gatherings of literati (Dorothy Parker and friends).

2 Café des Artistes
1 W.67th St. /877-3500

Noël Coward, Alexander Woollcott, et al., loved the hotel here. Diners at the Café still enjoy the sensuous nude nymphs in Howard Chandler Christy's murals.

3 Chumley's
86 Bedford St. (at Barrow St.)/675-4449

Bastion of Dos Passos, Lardner, Steinbeck and Joyce, the walls are smothered with dusty dust jackets. This was once a Village secret, now it's a little overknown, but still hard to find without a map.

4 Costello's
225 E.44th St. (bet. 2nd & 3rd Aves.)/599-9614

In it's fourth location, this itinerant is a favorite with journalists and literary sentimentalists seeking Thurber's original caricatures frescoed on the walls and Papa H.'s club. Also great for hamburger hunters.

5 Elaine's
1703 2nd Ave. (bet. E.88th & E.89th St.)/534-8103

Funky hangout for famous writers and other fast-track types, hosted by the indomitable Elaine herself.

6 Lion's Head
59 Christopher St. (at Sheridan Square)/929-0670

A writer/journalist/poet's haven with dust jackets, deadly wit and a distinctly Mailer/Breslin tang.

7 McSorley's Old Ale House
15 E.7th St. (off 3rd Ave.)/473-8800

Even the cobwebs are authentically antique in this ancient and overcrowded tavern. A favorite of Brendan Behan and other contemporary literary lushes (disguised as college students).

8 Pete's Tavern
129 E.18th St. (at Irving Pl.)/473-7676

A delightfully woody, time-warp tavern; you can sit in O. Henry's booth (where legend says he wrote "The Gift of the Magi") and drink in the 19th century ambience with your ale. Pleasant crowd, too.

9 21 Club
21 W.52nd St./582-7200

This was (as Jack & Charlie's Luncheon Club) the alternative venue for Parker's Round Table (see **The Algonquin**). It's still a magnet for the power elite with a discernible pecking order.

The West End Café
2911 Broadway (at W.113th St.)/666-8750

Famed focus for Kerouac, Ginsberg, Burroughs and the Beat writers of the '50s. Now it's a frisky student hangout and jazz nexus. Honestly basic.

The White Horse Tavern
567 Hudson St. (at W.11th St.)/243-9260

A veritable shrine for admirers of Mailer and Dylan Thomas (who drank himself into an early grave here and elsewhere in 1953). Too touristy for some, but evocative for others during the quieter hours.

LIVE MUSIC I

The Apollo *see UNUSUAL NIGHT SPOTS*

1 Asti
13 E.12th St. (off 5th Ave.)/741-9105
Moderate/Opera/all major
The star sings from center stage in the dining room, arias and all. On starless nights, the staff performs instead. Unmemorable food, but the rest can be fun!

2 Café Feenjon
117 MacDougal St. (bet. W.3rd & Bleecker Sts.)/254-3630
Moderate/Middle Eastern/no cards
A Middle East mishmash of entertainment, with everything from belly dancers to horahs, with crowd to match and some Saturday night laughs.

3 Café Marimba
1115 3rd Ave. (entrance on E.65th St.)/935-1161
Moderate/Mexican/Amex, DC
Authentic contemporary Mexican decor and entertainment with innovative delicacies. An unexpected and secluded delight.

4 The Cat Club
76 E.13th St. (bet. 4th Ave. & Broadway)/505-0090
Moderate/cov. varies/call ahead
Twilight Zone for Rock 'n' Roll freaks into hardcore. This is considered the top place for this kind of thing. So be warned and check first.

5 Dan Lynch
221 2nd Ave. (off E.14th St.)/473-8807
Inexpensive/no cards
This is a saloon serious about its deep down and dirty blues. Pussyfooters need not apply, 'cause it's deadly for the delicate. Just pass the pip cup.

6 Eagle Tavern
355 W.14th St. (at 9th Ave.)/924-0275
Inexpensive/$5 min./MC, V
Indubitably one of the oldest and wildest true Irish pubs in an appropriate neighborhood (slightly gentrified already) with matching Irish seisuns.

7 Hawaii Kai
1638 Broadway (at W.50th St.)/757-0900
Moderate/Polynesian/all major
Grass hut condo with shows to match. Very touristy trendy and popular with the after-theatre crowd.

8 Rasputin
371 W.46th St. (off 10th Ave.)/586-1860
Moderate/Amex, MC
Mad Russian, wild passion, Eastern European flavor and flair. For lingering and lounging in.

9 Rosie O'Grady's South
211 Pearl St. (off Maiden Lane)/424-7912
Inexpensive/all major
Packed-out pubby place where the Clancy Brothers and other dulcet-toned Irishmen sing a ditty or two and fiddle while you let it burn out on the dance floor, in your seat or in your heart.

Silverbird *see UNUSUAL NIGHT SPOTS*

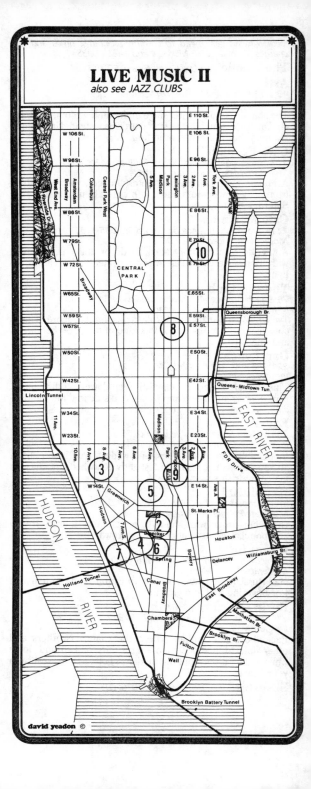

LIVE MUSIC II
also see JAZZ CLUBS

1 Abilene Café
359 2nd Ave. (at E.21st St.)/473-8908
Top cov. $15/no cards
Great late-night piano blues by Teo, hot when it gets cooking, and even edible food.

2 Bottom Line
15 W.4th St. (off Mercer St.)/228-6300
$10 cov./no cards
A Village tradition, going back to speakeasy days. Now a clean, comfortable institution with a wide variety of acts, bands and cabarets. Best bet is to call first.

3 Chelsea Place
147 8th Ave. (bet. W.17th & W.18th Sts.)/924-8413
Moderate/top cov. $20/all major
Look behind the antique-shop façade for a rockin' R&B dance spot and showcase with a very eclectic Chelsea, SoHo and downtown group.

4 Kenny's Castaways
157 Bleecker St. (at Thompson St.)/473-9870
Inexpensive/no cards
Occasionally fills up to its antlers with a rowdy crowd that gets down on rock 'n roll or folk songs, depending on the mood. Call first if you're fussy.

5 The Lone Star Café
61 5th Ave. (at E.13th St.)/242-1664
Moderate/top cov. $20/all major
Even hermit celebrities are occasionally drawn into this Wild-West saloon, with live acts straight from the top country charts. The giant lizard on the roof is a nice touch, too.

6 Rock & Roll Café
Bleecker and Thompson Sts./no phone
Inexpensive/no cards
Decorated with hub caps, posters and other appropriate auto-paraphernalia, the place rocks and rolls to live bands and occasional comedy.

7 S.O.B. (Sounds of Brazil)
204 Varick St. (at W.Houston St.)/243-4940
Moderate/all major
Rio de Janeiro on Varick. Menu and music match up to create this special surprise with live bands that make you swing your hips, samba, bossa nova and all.

8 Tommy Makem's Irish Pavilion
130 E.57th St. (off Lexington Ave.)/759-9040
Moderate/all major
An unpretentious pub, around for more than 20 years, visited by politicians, priests and power brokers who groove on the Irish bands that make you pause and listen. Eyes smile.

9 Tramps
125 E.15th St. (bet. 3rd Ave. & Irving Pl.)/777-5077
Inexpensive/no cards
Deep down Dixie, rock 'n' roll or rhythm 'n' blues, depending on the night, for a price that can't be beat, with burgers and brew on the side.

0 Wilson's
1444 1st Ave. (at E.75th St.)/861-0320
Inexpensive-moderate/Amex, DC
Always popular and always packed, Wilson's soft rock music mix keeps them coming back for more every time. The atmosphere is Victorian, but the mores are not!

PIANO ROOMS

1 The Algonquin Hotel/The Oak Room
59 W.44th St. (off 6th Ave.)/840-6800
Moderate/all major
Traditional, historical, romantic, and fail-safe. Also for the powerful and the seen-to-be-scene.

2 Arthur's Tavern
77 Grove St. (off 7th Ave. So.)/675-6879
Inexpensive/no cards
Very Village on a busy Village corner. Good company, good talk, good music, good fun and Mable Godwin ties it all together on weekends.

3 Broadway Baby
407 Amsterdam Ave. (bet. W.79th & W.80th Sts.)/724-6868
Moderate/Classic showtunes/Amex, MC, V
Tight, cozy and familiar, mainly because of the showtunes; friendly because of the laughter. A good West Side bet.

4 Café Carlyle
The Carlyle Hotel/35 E.76th St. (off Madison Ave.)/744-1600
Moderate/all major
Bobby Short's cool high-class act is purrfect. Very chic, very sophisticated, very Kennedy '60s.

5 Five Oaks
49 Grove St. (off 7th Ave. So.)/243-8885
Moderate/all major
A classic piano bar on a classic Village corner with an active social scene and some showtune sing-alongs.

6 Harry's Bar
The Helmsley Hotel
212 E.42nd St. (bet. 1st & 2nd Aves.)/490-8900
Moderate/all major
Excellent cocktail piano by Martin goes with a very chic upper crust crowd, over 30, well-heeled and Helmsley oriented. Check out the New York Bar at her Palace, too—it's piano in a Tiffany setting.

7 Le Vert Galant
109 W.48th St. (off 6th Ave.)/382-0022
Moderate-expensive/all major
One of the classiest and proper piano bars in the city, with heavy French accent and sophisticated flair here that makes the difference. You don't have far to go if you want to dine before or after, either—the food/service in the other room is excellent.

8 Mimi's
984 2nd Ave. (at E.52nd St.)/688-4692
Moderate/all major
Different from the norm, and that's why we like it. Open mike, open atmosphere, great and gutsy with a primo Italian menu and attitudes to match. The shenanigans at the piano are pure fun. No affectations here.

9 The Polo Lounge
The Westbury Hotel/15 E.69th St. (entrance on Madison, bet. E.68th & E.69th Sts.)/535-9141/Moderate/all major
So high-class as to be virtually unattainable, but access to the cool piano music is as simple as walking through the doors, past Prince Charles (sans Lady Di) and passing muster. Jacket and tie required.

SINGLES SPOTS

david yeadon ©

Amsterdam's on Amsterdam
428 Amsterdam Ave. (bet. W.80th & W.81st Sts.)/874-1377
Moderate/20-40/all major

Quite upmarket, suited and shoulder-padded. Lively till one, at least.

Arizona 206
206 E.60th St. (bet. 2nd & 3rd Aves.)/838-0440
Moderate/25-35/all major

Very availables here make no secret of seeking out what they want. Obvious as soon as you walk in the door, and most are good-looking. The southwestern food is noteworthy, too.

Bar Lui
625 Broadway (bet. Bleecker and Houston Sts.)/473-8787
Moderate/25 and up/Village, downtown mix/Amex, MC, V

Knows it's hot, gets scrumptiously scrunched on weekends. Success depends on you.

Cadillac Bar
15 W.21st St. (off 6th Ave.)/645-7220
Moderate/25 and up/yuppies from all over, preppies, too/Amex, MC, V

The hugest, hottest (not the best) Tex-Mex palace in town, where the main action is checking out the action; well-greased with free-flowing shots of tequila served wild and do it yourself graffiti, too.

Café Pacifico
384 Columbus Ave. (bet. W.78th & W.79th Sts.)/724-9187
Moderate/25 and up/very chic, some NY originals, mixed/all major cards

A peachy playpen with plenty of style 'n' stance and a fascinating mélange of international types and city slickers, so state your game upfront. Excellent for fueling the fires of desires.

Jim McMullen's
1341 3rd Ave. (at E.76th St.)/861-4700
Moderate/25 and up/from all over, mostly professionals/Amex

The male stallions here are looking hard, the ladies are too. Haute snobberie prevails (it's cool, where Pacifico is hot) and everyone is smart and snappy. Happy hunting.

The Limelight
47 W.20th St. (entrance on 6th Ave.)/807-7850
$15-20 cov./25 and up, city types, bridge & tunnel and tourists/Amex

Singles call it the "Slime" and all agree the action is constant—on the floor and at the bar. For those who can deal with high church decor while contemplating high jinks. This is one of a kind.

Lucy's Home for Retired Surfers
503 Columbus Ave. (at W.84th St.)/787-3009
Moderate/20's-40's/Amex

This place prides itself on its reputation for success in singling and mingling, pairing and sharing at incredible speeds. It's also a Gulf Coast knock-off and packs a decent blue margarita for this part of town.

Tuba City Truck Stop
1700 2nd Ave. (off E.88th St.)/996-6200
Inexpensive/young, mommy, young/all major

The East Side version of Lucy's, jammed like a can of sardines, so prowling is difficult and the noise level distracts from conversation. Make a hit, grab your partner and split. If consumation isn't of essence, you can always watch the playoffs.

TRADITIONAL TAVERNS
see also LITERARY WATERING HOLES

david yeadon ©

1 Billy's
948 1st Ave. (bet. E.52nd & E.53rd St.)/355-8920
The oldest family-owned restaurant in town, a casual neighborhood nexus offering above-average steaks and chops and the true feeling of old New York.

Bradley's *see JAZZ CLUBS*

2 Cedar Tavern
82 University Pl. (bet. E.11th & E.12th Sts.)/243-9355
Not as old as some, but charmingly basic all the same downstairs; with the airy sky-lit garden eatery upstairs.

Chumley's *see LITERARY WATERING HOLES*

Costello's *see LITERARY WATERING HOLES*

3 Fraunces Tavern
Broad and Pearl Sts./269-0144
Well-restored historical niche with evocative bar-restaurant and fascinating museum upstairs. Popular with visitors.

4 The Green Derby
994 2nd Ave. (bet. E.52nd & E.53rd Sts.)/688-1250
An almost overly Irish tavern with all the trimmings and genuine colleens, too.

5 Harvey's Chelsea Restaurant
108 W.18th St. (bet. 6th & 7th Aves.)/243-5644
A glowing tribute to Victorian pub decor complete with mahogany galore, fine etched glass and burnished brass—plus a decent Irish/American menu.

6 The Landmark Tavern
626 11th Ave. (at W.46th St.)/757-8595
This old longshoreman's refuge, with lovingly restored Irish-Victoriana decor, now attracts a well-heeled crowd of conventioneers and those looking for something a bit different.

7 Molly Malone's
287 3rd Ave. (bet. E.22nd & E.23rd Sts.)/725-8375
A real pubby Irish haven for nighttime camaraderie with stellar bartenders and always jovial company.

8 Old Town
45 E.18th St. (bet. Park Ave. & Broadway/529-6732
All that a real old NY tavern should be, with tin ceiling, booths, brass lamps and an eager young crowd. A welcome oasis off the flashy Fifth Ave. Spine.

9 Peter MacManus Café
152 7th Ave. (at W.19th St.)/929-9691
"The poor man's country club" is still offering an eclectic grouping of locals in a pleasantly frayed stained glass and mahogany setting.

10 P.J. Clarke's
915 3rd Ave. (at E.55th St.)/759-1650
Ancient high-energy, hard-drinking midtown focus, a true New York tavern for journalists, powerbrokers and celebrities. (There's also an odd clone in Macy's Cellar!).

11 Teacher's, Too
2271 Broadway (bet. W.81st & W.82nd Sts.)/362-4900
Pleasantly understated and companionable neighborhood niche with bulletin board, quiet conversation and a sense of going on forever.

UNUSUAL NIGHTSPOTS

W 106 St.
W 96 St.
W 86 St.
W 79 St.
W 72 St.
W 65 St.
W 59 St.
W 57 St.
W 50 St.
W 42 St.
W 34 St.
W 23 St.
W 14 St.

E 110 St.
E 106 St.
E 96 St.
E 86 St.
E 79 St.
E 72 St.
E 66 St.
E 59 St.
E 57 St.
E 50 St.
E 42 St.
E 34 St.
E 23 St.
E 14 St.

West End Ave.
Amsterdam
Columbus
Central Park West
5 Ave.
Madison
Park
Lexington
3 Ave.
2 Ave.
1 Ave.
York Ave.
Ave. A

Broadway

CENTRAL PARK

Riverside Dr.

HUDSON RIVER

EAST RIVER

Lincoln Tunnel
Holland Tunnel
Queens - Midtown Tun.
Queensborough Br.
Williamsburg Br.
Manhattan Br.
Brooklyn Br.
Brooklyn Battery Tunnel

11 Ave.
10 Ave.
9 Ave.
8 Ave.
7 Ave.
6 Ave.
5 Ave.
Madison
Park
Lexington
3 Ave.
2 Ave.
1 Ave.
FDR Drive

Greenwich
Hudson
Bleecker
Bowery
Houston
Spring
Delancey
Canal
Broadway
East Broadway
Chambers
Fulton
Wall
St. Marks Pl.

8 5 3 1 2 6 4 7

david yeadon ©

The Apollo
253 W.125th St. (east of Broadway)/749-5838
$5-$30 depending on the show/call ahead
Check out the bookings for the next few times you're in town. Wednesday night is Amateur Night and it's an unforgettable experience. Forget all those scare-stories about Harlem. Go for it.

1 Bill's Gay Nineties
57 E.54th St. (bet. Madison & Park Aves.)/355-0243
Moderate/all major
Music hall nostalgia served up with dinner and amusing entertainments, mostly for a conservative set with a penchant for the past.

2 Café Feenjon
117 MacDougal St. (bet. W.3rd & Bleecker Sts.)/254-3630
Moderate/no cards
Unusual because of the mix, the music, the shesh-besh, the chess, the comedy and the crowd. One of a kind on the whole island.

Café Pacifico *see SINGLES SPOTS*

3 Chippendale's
1110 1st Ave. (off E.61st St.)/935-6060/
Moderate/cov. varies/Amex
All sorts of good-looking guys take their clothes off and swing their hips at the faces of this straight, looking-for-thrills female crowd. As rowdy as ladies can get.

4 5 & 10, No Exaggeration
77 Greene St. (bet. Spring & Broome Sts.)/925-7414
Moderate/call ahead/all major
This is definitely not a run-of-the mill anything: restaurant, cabaret, antique shop, jewelry showcase, jazz and more, all run with moxie.

5 Jacqueline's
132 E.61st St. (bet. Park & Lexington Aves.)/838-4559
Moderate/all major
This tiny little Swiss restaurant is also the only champagne bar in the whole city, where a flute of top-quality champagne goes for a song. Delightful.

Jezebel's *see AMERICAN RESTAURANTS*

Peculier Pub
182 W.4th St. (bet. 6th & 7th Aves./691-8667
Inexpensive/no cards
Tiny, hole-in-the-wall haven for lovers of beer. Over 200 national selections here and a most convivial crowd.

7 Reggae Lounge
285 W.Broadway (off Varick St.)/266-4598
Cov. varies/no cards
Highly unusual security arrangements for a nightclub. . .it's as tight as El Al flying to Tel Aviv. . .with metal detectors, bag checks and pat-downs. Not without reason, either. The Latin heat and the reggae beat here sizzle, the crowd cooks and there's a Mardi Gras craziness about the whole place.

8 Silverbird
505 Columbus Ave. (bet. W.84th St. & W.85th St.)/877-7777
Moderate/no cards
One of a kind on the East or West Coasts. A Native American-Indian restaurant which doubles as a museum and shop for Native American handicrafts and art, as well as an educational outreach center. Beautifully done by Reuben Silverbird and his staff.

AFTERNOON TEAS

1 Carlyle Hotel
35 E. 76th St./744-1600

You expect the staff of this elegant edifice to offer the perquisites of a gracious tea, and they do. . .every afternoon in the muted red lobby. The high standards are carried over from the famed Café and are very evident in this daily ritual.

2 The Helmsley Palace
455 Madison Ave. (bet. E. 50th & E. 51st Sts.)/888-7000

Despite Leona's tedious ad campaign, her pretensions are realized. High tea in The Gold Room is so royal, one expects the Queen–her-majestic-self–to appear.

3 Hotel Intercontinental
111 E. 48th St. (bet. Lexington & Park Aves.)/755-5900

NEW YORK POST columnist Beth Fallon introduced us to this institution's high teas, and we're very glad she did. Formerly The Barclay, the lobby is as sumptuous, plush and rarified as a 19th century men's club. The house brand is often wonderfully pungent and available in take-home tins.

4 Hotel Pierre — Best
5th Ave. at 61st St./838-8000

Another spot to indulge visions of grandeur. The Rotunda tables are widely scattered to secure and ensure discreet secrecy. No overheard conversations here; instead, daydreams are evoked by the storybook murals and the savory scones. And if afternoon tea leaves you peckish, stay on for a sumptuous French dinner at the **Café Pierre**.

5 The King's Angel
119 E. 74th St. (bet. Park & Lexington Aves.)/879-4320

This, unbelievably, is the Parish House of The Church of The Resurrection, and the angel does exist. Her name is Ruth Wiltshire, the parish priest's British secretary, and for the most nominal sum in town, she will serve up a spread you won't soon forget. Lord love her shortbread. . .we surely do!

6 Mayfair Regent Hotel
Park Ave. at E. 65th St./288-0800

The brass service cart and the lissome lassies in traditional English serving garb go far to recapture the tradition's heyday.

7 The Plaza Hotel
5th Ave. at 59th St./759-3000

The famed Palm Court is the site in this venerable hostelry, and while we have a warm spot in our hearts for it, we find the volume of pedestrian traffic going to and fro quite distracting, diminishing the serenity demanded by the customary rites.

8 The Stanhope Hotel
995 5th Ave. (at E. 81st St.)/288-5800

The entire food service area has been renovated, and with it, the notions for afternoon tea. Le Salon is the designated area for assignations, and is cozy and intimate. Only 30 persons can be accommodated at one sitting. The waitresses are Frenchily clad, the captain wears tails and makes his guests feel very much at home.

9 The Waldorf Astoria
Park Ave. (at E. 50th St.)/872-4818

Come to the art deco Cocktail Terrace, overlooking the famous lobby, and sample the Americanized version of this veddy British amenity.

COFFEE HOUSES

Map labels:

W 106 St.
W 96 St.
W 86 St.
W 79 St.
W 72 St.
W 65 St.
W 59 St.
W 57 St.
W 50 St.
W 42 St.
W 34 St.
W 23 St.
W 14 St.

E 110 St.
E 106 St.
E 96 St.
E 86 St.
E 79 St.
E 72 St.
E 65 St.
E 59 St.
E 57 St.
E 50 St.
E 42 St.
E 34 St.
E 23 St.
E 14 St.

Riverside Dr.
West End Ave.
Broadway
Amsterdam
Columbus
Central Park West
5 Ave.
Madison
Park
Lexington
3 Ave.
2 Ave.
1 Ave.
York Ave.
Ave. A

CENTRAL PARK

Broadway

11 Ave.
10 Ave.
9 Ave.
8 Ave.
7 Ave.
6 Ave.
5 Ave.
Madison
Park Ave. S.
Lexington
3 Ave.
2 Ave.
1 Ave.

HUDSON RIVER
EAST RIVER
FDR Drive

Lincoln Tunnel
Queensborough Br.
Queens - Midtown Tun.

Greenwich
Hudson
Gay St.
Bleecker
Houston
St. Marks Pl.
Spring
Bowery
Delancey
Williamsburg Br.
Canal
Broadway
East Broadway
Holland Tunnel
Chambers
Manhattan Br.
Brooklyn Br.
Fulton
Wall
Brooklyn Battery Tunnel

david yeadon ©

1 Biagio's
309 E.89th St. (bet. 1st & 2nd Aves.)/534-3248
Inexpensive/Daily 11-2 a.m./Amex, DC
We'll confess, we melt for a good mousse. The name attracted us and the desserts keep us coming back. The Mochaccino and pecan pie are also addictive. Heaven help our waistlines!

2 Café Biondo
141 Mulberry St. (at Hester St.)/226-9285
Moderate/M-F noon-midnight, S&Su noon-2/no cards
A welcome addition to the Little Italy scene, quickly becoming a favorite on this fabled street. It has the same classy ambience as a new car, and a festive atmosphere prevails—especially out under the umbrellas on warm nights.

3 Caffé Reggio and Café Corner
119 MacDougal St. (at Minetta Lane)/475-9557
Inexpensive/M-Th noon-2 a.m., F-S 'til 3, cl. Su/no cards
The oldest cafe in Greenwich Village, with minuscule tables, delightful sandwiches and friendly service, attracting the elbow-patched crowd, New Wave romantics, and old-time Villagers. Nearby is cafe corner with **Café Borgia**, **Le Figaro** and **Caffé Dante**, all venerable Village fixtures.

4 Caffé Roma
385 Broome St. (at Mulberry St.)/226-8413
Moderate/8-midnight, daily/no cards
This is no plastic palace for pasta peckers it's the real McCoy. We like this neighborhood, and lots of other folks feel the same way, so be prepared for a wait on weekends and holidays. Desserts are divine, and the pastry is sold on a cash & carry basis, too.

5 Café Vivaldi
32 Jones St. (off Bleecker St.)/929-9384
Moderate/Daily 10-2 a.m./no cards
Come to relax; it's peaceful and green, especially springtimes. Bring the Sunday papers, order the tostini, and ignore your watch.

6 The Cloister Café
238 E.9th St. (bet. 2nd & 3rd Aves.)/777-9128
Moderate/Su-Th noon-12:30 a.m., F&S till 1:30/no cards
Their garden motif works very nicely in the brick courtyard. Café au lait is their trademark—and should be. The East Village, incidentally, particularly along St. Marks Pl., is now packed with coffee house in the West Village tradition of twenty years ago. Check it out. We especially enjoy **Life Café** on Tompkins Square (which is more than a coffee house) and **Café Orlin** on St. Marks, too.

7 Cornelia St. Café
29 Cornelia St. (off 6th Ave.)/929-9869
Moderate/Daily, 8 a.m.-2 a.m./no cards
A deservedly popular institution and happy hybrid with a reputation for excellent food from an eclectic menu, poetry readings and a variety of entertainments.

8 Hungarian Pastry Shop
111th St. and Amsterdam Ave./860-4230
Inexpensive/Su-Th 9 a.m.-10:30, F&S 'til 11:30/no cards
A truly European Café in a neighborhood that has a very Old World flavor, directly across the street from St. John the Divine, with a clientele that crawls out of Columbia classrooms for coffee served with pastry, politics and philosophy.

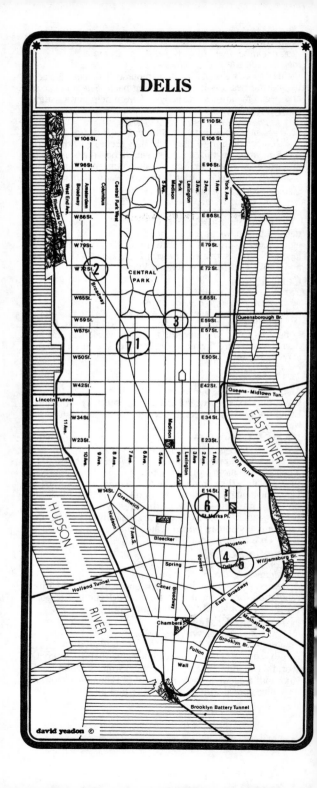

DELIS

david yeadon ©

1 Carnegie Deli
854 7th Ave. (bet. W.54th & W.55th Sts.)/757-2245
The comics in "Broadway Danny Rose" weren't noshing here by accident. This is the archetypal NY deli and has always been popular with the showbiz crowd, and others who enjoy Catskill kosher style (but non-kosher) goodies, like a pastrami on club with a side.

2 Fine & Shapiro
138 W.72nd St. (bet. Broadway & Columbus Ave.)/877-2874
Under rabbinical supervision
The kosher deli of renown throughout the town. You name it, they've got it. . .from gefilte fish, chicken soup and chopped liver to pareve (non-dairy) melt-in-your-mouth butter cookies imported from Phibbleberry's in Teaneck, all at appealing prices.

3 Kaplan's at The Delmonico
59 E.59th St. (bet. Park & Madison Aves.)/755-5959
Another perennial, with a loyal following that eats-in or takes out. The cold cuts beckon and don't disappoint. Splurge on a "Volga Boatman"—cream cheese, velvety Novie and sable on a bagel.

4 Katz's Deli
205 E. Houston St. (off Ludlow St.)/254-2246
A bonafide NY deli (not like the one on W.57th) which has been around since the beginning of forever, with bonafide characters on both sides of the counter, who'll debate the virtues of pastrami over corned beef and then stuff themselves on dogs with the works and celery soda. Anyone here ordering anything on white bread will be laughed out the door to the Upper East Side. Club and rye is where it's at, and mayo is for tuna and potato salad only. Heartburn heaven. Enjoy.

5 Schmulka Bernstein's
135 Essex St. (off Rivington St.)/473-3900
Under rabbinical supervision
If you want to eat authentic kosher deli with an authentic group in the authentic neighborhood. If you're there, you can't beat Schmulka's and you'll also want to sample the first kosher Chinese food made in America, even before **Moshe Peking, Shang-Chai.** For a real feel of Lower East Side, try Saturday nights, around 11.

6 Second Ave. Deli
156 2nd Ave. (at E.10th St.)/677-0606
The patent on chopped liver (with onions, radish and schmaltz) goes to **Sammy's Roumanian** (which isn't a deli and charges top dollar; see UNUSUAL RESTAURANTS), but these guys knock off a close second for a lot less moolah. The mushroom barley soup is like Ma makes, thick and full of barley, beef and mushrooms that have been simmered for centuries on the back burner.

7 The Stage Deli
834 7th Ave. (bet. W.53rd & W.54th Sts.)/245-7850
A bit glitzy, but that's the idea. Its proximity to the major midtown hotels ensures popularity with tourists who will visit because of what they heard. The sandwiches named for stars are their glory. Our favorite last time was the "Shecky Greene," a mountain of corned beef, pastrami and swiss cheese.

HAMBURGER HAVENS

W 106 St. / W 96 St. / W 86 St. / W 79 St. / W 72 St. / CENTRAL PARK / W 65 St. / W 59 St. / W 57 St. / W 50 St. / W 42 St. / Lincoln Tunnel / W 34 St. / W 23 St. / W 14 St.

E 110 St. / E 106 St. / E 96 St. / E 86 St. / E 79 St. / E 72 St. / E 65 St. / E 59 St. / E 57 St. / E 50 St. / E 42 St. / E 34 St. / E 23 St. / E 14 St.

Riverside Dr. / West End Ave. / Broadway / Amsterdam / Columbus / Central Park West / 5 Ave. / Madison / Park / Lexington / 3 Ave. / 2 Ave. / 1 Ave. / York Ave.

Queensborough Br. / Queens - Midtown Tun.

11 Ave. / 10 Ave. / 9 Ave. / 8 Ave. / 7 Ave. / 6 Ave. / 5 Ave. / Park / Madison / Lexington / 3 Ave. / 2 Ave. / 1 Ave. / FDR Drive / Ave. A

EAST RIVER

Greenwich / Hudson / 7 Ave. S. / Bleecker / Spring / Canal / Broadway / Bowery / Houston / Delancey / St. Marks Pl. / East Broadway / Williamsburg Br.

Holland Tunnel / Chambers / Fulton / Wall / Manhattan Br. / Brooklyn Br.

HUDSON RIVER

Brooklyn Battery Tunnel

david yeadon ©

1 Broome Street Bar
363 W.Broadway (at Broome St.)/925-2086

We bet O. Henry would've loved this SoHo melting pot. It's chock-full of local color with a lively clientelle of artists and writers.

Costello's *see LITERARY WATERING HOLES*

2 Hamburger Harry's
157 Chambers St. (bet. W.Broadway & Greenwich St.)/247-4446
145 W.45th St. (bet. Broadway & 6th Ave.)/840-0566

There's no total unanimity on these brisk, modern burger havens, and the high prices can be a surprise, but we enjoy the mesquite broiling and have never been disappointed.

3 Jackson Hole Wyoming
1633 2nd Ave. (at E.85th St.)/737-8788
and other Manhattan locations

This small collection of eateries has put an interesting spin on the traditional NY coffee shop. Their unabashed specialty is hamburger, and burger lovers rank them as among the best anywhere. Twelve varieties are available, but don't pass up the sauteed mushrooms and the omelettes. Blow-up posters of the West provide some mood, but the real distraction is the diverse crowd.

4 J.G. Melon
1291 3rd Ave. (at E.74th St.)/650-1310
340 Amsterdam Ave. (at W.76th St.)/874-8291

A noble purveyor of the venerable "bar burger," a breed of patty that's handmolded (and therefore bulky and uneven), served on a paper plate barely bigger than its bun. Splendid.

5 The Landmark Tavern
626 11th Ave. (at W.46th St.)/757-8595

We love this mahogany and leaded-glass ark founded in 1868. It's in danger of becoming trendy since Hell's Kitchen became Convention Center territory. But to us, it will always remain a gin mill with class. Some like to munch their burgers in the antiquey dining room upstairs. We'll stick to ordering ours in the bar.

6 Martell's
1649 3rd Ave. (at E.83rd St.)/861-6110

On the East Side, another burger is waiting—in front of one of the few fireplaces in winter or out on the patio in summer. Pump some quarters in the super jukebox. Everything tastes better with good ole '50s rock and roll.

7 O'Neal's Baloon
48 W.63rd St. (at Amsterdam Ave.)/399-2353

Though this establishment always seemed a little touristy to us, we won't deny they serve up a mighty good burger, and we appreciate their patience when we design our own garnishes. Ideal for pre-post Lincoln Center performances.

8 P.J. Clarke's
915 3rd Ave. (at E.55th St.)/759-1650

One of NY's vital organs—albeit too vitally mobbed during happy hour. A perfect evocation of a 19th century Irish saloon, right down to the sawdust on the floor—a perfect time machine. Hunker down with your burger in the marvelously murky backroom and have some spinach salad, too. Or join the crowd at the bar, if you can steal a stool.

ICE CREAM SHOPS

david yeadon ©

1 Agora
1550 3rd Ave. (at E.87th St.)/369-6983
As close to an old fashioned NY ice cream parlor as you can get. Try a soda in this gingerbread fantasy, then check out the adjacent boutique. *see also Serendipity in UNUSUAL RESTAURANTS*

2 Café Della Palma
327 Columbus Ave. (bet. W.75th & W.76th Sts.)/713-5558
Wonderful selection of Italian ice creams and sherbets, including several surprising flavors.

3 Dmitri's Café
156 Spring St. (at W.Broadway)/334-9239
A dessert landmark in SoHo, featuring Vermont's trendy Ben & Jerry's ice cream and delicious pastries.

4 Gelato Modo
464 Columbus Ave. (at W.82nd St.)/663-0942
744 Broadway (at Astor Pl.)/475-1166
Sorbeti spoken here—and how! With high fruit content in all the offerings, it can be argued that these treats are good for you.

5 Häagen-Dazs
1012 2nd Ave. (bet. E.53rd & E.54th Sts.)/355-1244
and other Manhattan locations
For our money, this is the best commercial ice cream in town. A pint from the grocer's freezer is as good as you get hand-dipped.

6 Minter's Ice Cream Kitchen
Pier 17, South Street Seaport/608-2037
A gild-the-lily operation, what with all the candies, cookies and fruit fragments one can use for embellishing the creamy base.

7 New York Ice Cream Co.
113 7th Ave. So. (bet. W.10th & Christopher Sts.)/741-5061
The city's hometown brand, and why not? Primarily a wholesaler, whose clients include the poshest uptown hotels, the products are worth sampling on the premises or in one of the many gourmet outlets they service.

8 Peppermint Park
666 5th Ave. (at W.53rd St.)/581-5938
1225 1st Ave. (at E.66th St.)/288-5054 and other locations
Bring the kids and try one of the sundaes at the bright white and green pleasure pit. It's always like a Saturday afternoon in July here.

9 San Ambroeus
1000 Madison Ave. (at E.77th St.)570-2211
An intriguing uptown hybrid, featuring menus for all three meals of the day, plus Italian ices to rival their lower-Manhattan counterparts—in every way but price.

10 Sedutto's
946 2nd Ave. (bet. E.50th & E. 51st Sts.)/980-3532 and other locations
Like Haagen-Dazs, this is a make-believe import of high quality which eschews the lamentable trend toward those awful, ersatz "soft" ice cream concoctions.

11 Steve's Ice Cream
286 Columbus Ave. (bet. W.74th & W.75th Sts.)/874-9348
and other locations.
Lord, how those yuppies love to scream for this ice cream! Cavity-encouraging garnishes available here in abundance.

PIZZA

1 Arturo's
106 W.Houston St. (off Thompson St.)/677-3980
Brick oven pizza that people claim is the best in the city.
Don't be shocked when your waiter bursts into song at the
open mike. This is one happy place.

2 Famous Ray's Pizza in The Village
465 6th Ave. (at W.11th St.)/243-2253
Forget all those other Original Ray's around town. They're
unrelated to this staunch pieman and couldn't come close to
carrying his crust. Cheese lovers should (and probably do)
flock here for the heaps of mozzarella on the slices. You can't
miss it—the crowd usually swarms out on the sidewalk.

3 Fiorello's
1900 Broadway (off W.64th St.)/595-5330
NEW YORK MAGAZINE anointed this as the best in town,
and we won't debate. We're frankly not interested in choosing one champ; the worst we ever had was pretty good. The
namesake pie here is a winner, what with its pungent goat
cheese and basil sauce.

4 Freddy and Pepe's Gourmet Pizza
101 W.68th St. (bet. Columbus Ave. & Broadway)/496-6909
Purists beware. They load it up with every topping
imaginable—broccoli, fried eggplant, even a seafood smorgasbord of squid, clams and mussels. While we agree there's
always room for plain pie, we like their style.

5 John's
278 Bleecker St. (at 7th Ave.)/243-1680
Tight and tiny, it's one of the Village's favorite pizza haunts
for an inexpensive but highly satisfying parlay. Come for a
meal, 'cause they don't serve single slices. And love that jukebox. Also a recent uptown version at E.64th and 1st Ave.,
935-2895.

6 Mezzaluna
1295 3rd Ave. (off E.74th St.)/535-9600
Okay, okay, so they aren't really a pizza parlor, and they're
not cheap, and they're trendy. But the pizzas are prime and
among the leaders.

7 PizzaPiazza
785 Broadway (at E.10th St.)/505-0977
Deep-dish pizza is still an innovation for NYorkers (especially
those who've never been to Chicago), and it's the specialty
here. Bring the Rolaids and order a gut-buster with everything (the usual, plus onions, zucchini, broccoli and three
cheeses). Aaah, such bliss, such overindulgence! There's a
full bar, too.

8 SoHo Kitchen and Bar
103 Greene St. (at Prince St.)/925-1866
Anyplace where you can eat crispy, spicy pizza with virtually
any accent and wash it down with something from a 100-plus
wine list or a dozen draft beers, is a find and a half. Expansion may spoil a good thing, but we can't help wishing management would open another uptown.

9 Tom's Pizzeria
510 Columbus Ave. (bet. W.84th & W.85th Sts.)/877-6954
A few years ago, on a gray February day that chilled to the
bone, a health food fanatic introduced us to Tom's whole
wheat crust. We were skeptical going in and converted going
out. It's chewy, flavorful and offers a nutritional bonus. (White
flour dough is available for the unrepentant.)

SIDEWALK CAFES

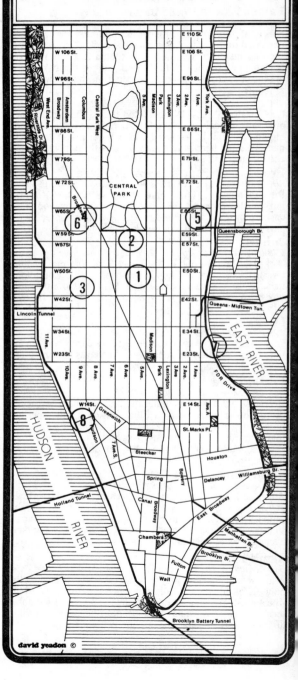

david yeadon ©

1 American Festival Café
20 W.50th St. (at Rockefeller Center)/246-6699
Moderate/all major
This sunny spot materializes Brigadoonish-fashion in the warm weather months, and the Rockefeller ice rink setting makes it one of the most delightful al fresco eateries in town. Dine fume-free beneath Prometheus' golden presence.

2 Café de la Paix
The St. Moritz Hotel
Central Park So. at 6th Ave./755-5800
Moderate/all major
Don't let its reputation as a tourist trap dissuade you. Its outdoor tables, pianist and delightful views of Central Park's midtown perimeter are a classic combination-actually quite Parisian.

3 Curtain Up!
402 W.43rd St. (at 9th Ave.)/564-7272
Moderate/all major
We've spent many an hour on this breezy patio (part of the Manhattan Plaza artists' colony), sipping their generous snifters of cognac and contemplating our place in the universe. Nonartist civilians are welcome too. Come see the whole neighborhood's spirited rejuvenation.

4 Fountain Café
Lincoln Center Plaza
Broadway at W.64th St./874-7000
Inexpensive/all major
Another one of the city's blessed grace notes. Come at lunchtime and enjoy one of their whole-grain sandwiches or pasta salads. In the evening, sip wine and watch the opera patrons and concert-goers stroll by. Very centering for the spirit.

5 Maxwell's Plum
1181 1st Ave. (at E.64th St.)/628-2100
Expensive/all major
A popular bistro, not insulted by the term "single's bar." The pace is a bit frantic at times, but now and again that can be stimulating.

6 The Saloon
1920 Broadway (at W.64th St.)/874-1500
Moderate/all major
Not by our definition, but a worthy candidate, nonetheless. The servers-on-roller-skates is a bit cute, but it certainly speeds up deliveries. Come and linger even if all you want is coffee. They really don't mind!

7 The Water Club
500 E.30th St. (at the East River)/683-3333
Very expensive/all major
Construing the East River as a sidewalk, this moored barge is a worthy inclusion. Whether inside or topside, the view is hypnotically relaxing as only water can be. Some think the menu is overpriced given the rather ordinary contents, but no one's objecting to their drinks.

8 The White Horse Tavern
567 Hudson St. (at W.11th St.)/243-9260
Moderate/no credit cards
This one really feels like a landmark and is still thick with a history of literary tipplers, and Dylan Thomas' antics. It's one of our favorite village hangouts, too, and we can endure its occasional over-popularity.

BAKERIES

1 Bonté Patisserie
1316 3rd Ave. (bet. E.75th & E.76th Sts.)/535-2360
Those who subscribe to Marie Antoinette's proclamation,
"Let them eat cake," will feel perfectly at home here, where
so many magnificent glitterati wedding cakes have been con-
structed. Try the Grand Marnier buttercream.

2 Colette
1136 3rd Ave. (bet. E.66th & E.67th Sts.)/988-2605
Rave notices for the French delights—brimming tarts, light-
as-air croissants, the best bavaroise on the Upper East Side
and custardy quiche.

3 Delices de Guy Pascal
1231 Madison Ave. (at E.89th St.)/289-5300
939 1st Ave. (bet. E.51st & E. 52nd Sts.)/371-4144
Two popular stores, plus a **Zabar** location,all known for light
'n' luscious croissants, tarts and brioches served to go or to
stay in their delightfully unpretentious cafés.

4 Dumas Patisserie
1330 Lexington Ave. (bet. E.88th & E.89th Sts.)/369-3900
Authentic and superior French pastry, accented by light-as-
feather croissants and superb mousse cake. Real men eat
Dumas' quiche, too.

5 Kramer's
1643 2nd Ave. (bet. E.85th & E.86th Sts.)/535-5955
Another Yorkville gem. The butter and chocolate cookies are
city-famous, and the mouthwatering pies are always made
with seasonal fruits. Try the petit fours.

6 Patisserie Lanciani
271 W.4th St. (at Perry St.)/929-0730
177 Prince St. (at Thompson St.)/477-2788
The proprietary pair here prepared the Plaza's pastry in-
house and now do their own thing. The éclairs are excellent,
as are most of their creations; the cappuccino is outstanding,
and you may take your refreshments to your café tables.

7 San Ambroeus
1000 Madison Ave. (bet. E.77th & E.78th Sts.)/570-2211
An aromatic outpost of the Milan original with diversity in
diet-destroying window displays of cakes, excellent gelatos
(try the hazelnut rum raisin) and tantalizing arrays of savories
& banini. Expensive though.

8 Veniero Pasticceria
342 E.11th St. (bet. 1st & 2nd Aves.)/674-7264
Just what you hope to find in the funky East Village—an exquisite Italian niche brimming with displays of pastries and
sugary delights in a lovely little café with soda fountain chairs.

9 William Greenberg, Jr.'s Bakery
1100 Madison Ave. (bet. E.82nd & E.83rd Sts.)/744-0304
1377 3rd Ave. (bet. E.78th & E.79th Sts.)/876-2255
912 7th Ave. (bet. W.57th & W.58th Sts.)/307-5930
Loaded with traditional coffee cakes and layers, cookies and
the other "American" things, but they also create European
delights like mini puff pastries and turnovers with such splendid finesse, friends have been known to swoon over a morsel
of schnecken and beg for the brownies.

BUTCHERS

david yeadon ©

1 Balducci's
424 6th Ave. (bet. W.9th & W.10th Sts.)/673-2600
This is one of our most preferred butchers. Their meats are every bit as savory as any specialists' selection; the game and bird offerings are also first-rate. Besides, it's one of the city's best gourmet shops.

2 Basior Schwartz Pork Store
421 W.14th St. (bet. 9th & 10th Aves.)/929-5368
If you don't mind the lurid neighborhood (now under gentrification), this outlet and the Washington Market (the city's wholesale meat district) are worth investigating. This particular shop is very accommodating to retail buyers who pay the same low discount rates.

3 Esposito & Sons Pork Store
500 9th Ave. (at W.38th St.)/279-3298
A popular entry on 9th Ave.'s "Butcher's Row," this second generation concern produces some of the best sausages in town. Their cold cuts, prosciutto and suckling pig are highly prized by gourmets in the know.

Jefferson Market
455 6th Ave. (at W.10th St.)/675-2277
Like Balducci's, this edifice holds an extraordinary array of gastronomic delights underscored by the expansive meat department. (Oh, for a fat-melting pill and a key to the door!)

5 Kurowycky Meats
124 1st Ave. (bet. E.7th & E.8th Sts.)/477-0344
Another example of why immigration has made America great. This Ukrainian enterprise includes a smokehouse which produces some of the richest-tasting cured hams and meats imaginable. Try a slice of the kielbasi!

6 Lobel Brothers' Prime Meats
1096 Madison Ave. (at E.82nd St.)/737-1372
As the address indicates, they'll lighten your wallet considerably—especially compared to some of the others on this list. But the quality is beyond reproach and the stock of more exotic fare (buffalo, venison, etc.) is a plus if pennies are of no concern.

7 Ottomanelli Brothers
1549 York Ave. (at E.82nd St.)/772-7900
Strong on game (wild boar, grouse) and long on service (they deliver), they also sell ready-to-serve sauces and such, keeping their East Side clientele very happy.

8 Regent Foods
1174 Lexington Ave. (bet. E.80th & E.81st Sts.)/288-2800
A terrific grocery store with a good meat department—all cuts are well-trimmed and there's usually an extensive selection of fresh game birds.

9 Schaller & Weber
1654 2nd Ave. (bet. E.85th & E.86th Sts.)/879-3047
Yorkville's favorite butcher creates all the wonderful handmade sausages and cold cuts you'd expect, plus offering all the prime beef, pork and poultry you could want. Pride, precision and tradition are the hallmarks here.

0 Washington Beef Company
573 9th Ave. (at W.41st St.)/563-0200
Try this sprawling spot if you have a freezer to fill or a mob to feed. Their prices are wholesale and they encourage bulk buying.

CHOCOLATIERS

david yeadon ©

1 Au Chocolat
Bloomingdale's (E.59th St. & Lexington Ave.)/705-2953
As is the case with the rest of Bloomie's, all name brands (and some obscure homemade originals) are boxed and waiting for you. A connoisseur's delight.

2 Chocolates by M
61 W.62nd St. (bet. Broadway & Columbus Ave.)/307-0777
Very expensive and very intriguing range of dipped everythings in wonderfully rich chocolates—take your pick and take a thick wallet.

3 Godiva Chocolatier
701 5th Ave. (off 55th St.)/593-2845
These elegantly packaged chocolates are considered by many to be the best and most prestigious of all. (Haute snob appeal, here.) The proximity to Tiffany's doesn't hurt their reputation as the "Tiffany's" of confection shops, although some claim declining quality.

4 Le Chocolatier Manon
827 Madison Ave. (at E.71st St.)/288-8088
If Godiva is Tiffany, then Manon is Cartier. The truffles are unexcelled—as are some of the prices.

5 Li-Lac Chocolates
120 Christopher St. (off Bleecker St.)/242-7374
We love the sense of handmade tradition and atmosphere dating back to 1923. The fudge is simply sinful.

Mondel Chocolates
2913 Broadway (at W.114th St.)/864-2111
Any candymaker who promotes chocolate with a low-fat content should be canonized, so the shop is a shrine and we worship here regularly.

6 Neuchatel
1369 6th Ave. (bet. W.55th & W.56th Sts. and other locations)/489-9320
Swiss delights from their new Pennsylvania chocolate factory, all prominently displayed in four Manhattan stores, including The Plaza. Wonderful truffles, exotic sculptures, and Paris-designed packaging.

7 Perugina
636 Lexington Ave. (at E.54th St.)/688-2490
Excellent Italian chocolates from the Perugina factory, featuring their beloved 'baci' chocolate kisses with the romantic notes and 'gianduia'—a beautiful blend of milk chocolate and hazelnut cream. Superb seasonal packaging, too.

8 St. Moritz
506 Madison Ave. (off E.52nd St.)/486-0265
Kron Chocolate reigns here. There are also many well-executed chocolate sculptures on the shelves—busts, cars, and even computers. They do custom designs, too, for a price, but samples are not unheard of for well-heeled wanderers.

9 Teuscher Chocolates of Switzerland
25 E.61st St./751-8482
620 5th Ave. (at Rockefeller Center)/246-4416
Each week they receive a fresh, mouthwatering shipment from Zurich, the chocolate Mecca of the universe. Beware the champagne truffle, their pride and joy. . .and don't say we didn't warn you!

GENERAL GOURMET SHOPS

1 Balducci's
424 6th Ave. (bet. W.9th & W.10th Sts./672-2600
A Greenwich Village mecca that still looks, feels and smells like the 1916 original Mom 'n' Pop store. Superior produce and prices that are sometimes lower than you'd expect from a top-of-the-line-tradition.

2 Bloomingdale's
1000 3rd Ave. (at E.59th St.)/705-2958
Short on service, long on lines and high on prices, but still a great selection of eat 'n' run goodies in fragmented departments for "grazing" yuppies out to lunch. Excellent bakery, too, featuring their own breads plus a wide selection from other top NY patisseries.

3 Dean and Deluca
121 Prince St. (bet. Greene & Wooster Sts.)/431-1691
Expensive but popular with SoHo residents and swarms of gallery-goers. Check out their selection of esoteric produce (the babiest of baby veggies up front) and wonderful range of unusual kitchenware.

4 E.A.T.
1064 Madison Ave. (bet. E.80th & E.81st Sts.)/879-4017
The gourmet store NYorkers love to hate, run by Eli Zabar. While it suffers from chronic overpricing, arrogant and brusque service, they have a knack of finding impossibly delicious foods out of season. If it gets to be too much, visit their friendlier gift shop next door.

5 Fraser-Morris
931 Madison Ave. (at E.74th St.)/988-6700
1264 3rd Ave. (at E.73rd St.)/288-7716
Notable assortments of candy, charcuteries and cheeses are hallmarks here. Ditto their gift baskets and sandwiches to go. Bring your wallet—the fat one.

6 Jefferson Market
455 6th Ave. (bet. W.10 & W.11th Sts.)/675-2277
While all the standard stock is here, their strength is in the impeccable selection of fresh fish and meats. What they lack in bargain prices, they make up in exemplary, solicitous service.

7 Macy's Cellar
Broadway and Herald Square/695-4400
A controversial best, but the range is extensive and it's a lot of fun. If you don't want to traipse all over town for your delicacies, everything from sweets to meats is here in a convenient one-stop-shop.

8 Maison Glass
52 E.58th St. (bet. Madison & Park Aves.)/755-3316
Old World charm and service with a wealth of goodies from Britain, France, Germany and exotic places. There's also a boggling array of caviar, smoked meats, fish and oh-so-lovely chutneys.

9 Zabar's
2245 Broadway at W.80th St./787-2000
Don't come here for lunch, there are no eat-in facilities and they frown on making sandwiches. For smoked fish, salads and other deli specialities, however, they're hard to beat, and the kitchenware is overwhelming. They also seem to be capable of endless expansion.

GOURMET-TO-GO

david yeadon ©

Note: We've selected stores specializing in the preparation and sale of gourmet dishes. See also GENERAL GOURMET SHOPS and SPECIALIZED GOURMET SHOPS

1 Chelsea Foods
198 8th Ave. (at W.20th St.)/691-3948

In just four years, this emporium has carved out a permanent niche in the delectables market. When we saw the sushi, we conceded they could manage anything, even occasional cooking demonstrations.

2 Fisher and Levy Food Shop
1026 2nd Ave. (at E.54th St.)/832-3880

This friendly, fast-track duo have created a sparkling shop, dedicated to the proposition that all foraging preppies are created equally fast-paced. Start with the salad bar and build yourself a splendid repast faster here than anywhere.

3 Grace's Marketplace
1237 3rd Ave. (bet. E.71st St. & E.72nd St.)/288-0501

A lovely well-organized newcomer (from a venerable family) offering exemplary selections of cheeses, gourmet-to-go dishes, pastas, vegetables and an already outstanding catering service. Welcome!

4 Les Trois Petits Cochons
453 Greenwich St. (So. of Canal)/219-1555

It means Three Little Pigs, because it's the market they were looking for. (Who'll argue?) Pâtés are the house specialties, and they justifiably receive accolades for peerless texture and depth of flavor. The "instant picnic" concession is also a brilliant idea.

5 Mangia
54 W.56th St. (bet. 5th & 6th Aves.)/582-3061

We like their sourdough bread sandwiches and the fact that you don't need to buy a shelfload of goods to qualify for delivery. The homemade baked goods are fine, and although we haven't tried it out, they suggest letting them pack a meal for your next flight out-of-town.   Anything to avoid airline agonies!

6 Russ & Daughters
179 E. Houston St. (bet. Allen & Orchard Sts.)/475-4880

Long live multi-generational Mom 'n' Pop shops like this one. They've cornered the market on fancy fish items—lake sturgeon and all that lovely caviar. The party platters (assorted appetizers) are popular among the regulars.

7 Silver Palate
274 Columbus Ave. (at W.73rd St.)/799-6340

How does this diminutive store-front support the extraordinary supply and demand? With catering, cooking, mail orders, book-writing, gift packaging and schmoozing, you'd think they'd need a thousand times more floor space. Their basket combos make for prime up-scale picnics.

8 William Poll
1051 Lexington Ave. (bet. E.74th & E.75th Sts.)/288-0501

William is now retired, but wife Christine and son Stanley still use recipes tested for over 60 years for that famous moussaka, coq au vin, and dozens of other appetizers and entrees. In addition, they make their own chocolates, keep the best smoked salmon in town and run an excellent retail section.

9 Word of Mouth
1012 Lexington Ave. (bet. E.72nd & E.73rd Sts.)/734-9483

They have no catering service, which enhances their credo about "homecooking." The menu is eclectic, esoteric and full of surprises. This is one very epicurean Mouth!

GREENMARKETS

David Yeadon ©

Note: The Council on Environment of New York City, since its founding in 1976, has promoted the idea of "green-markets," open-air stalls where regional farmers can sell their produce at specific times and locations around the city and the boroughs. Here's where they are in Manhattan, from south-north. (Call 566-0990 for the latest information.)

1 Southbridge Towers
Beekman & Pearl Sts.
Saturdays from June 1-December 21

2 City Hall
Municipal Building South
Fridays from June 28-November 22

3 World Trade Center
Church Street
Tuesdays & Thursdays from June 4-December 24

4 Independence Plaza
Greenwich & Harrison
Wednesdays & Saturdays from June 8-December 21

5 1st St. and 1st Ave.
Sundays from June 16-November 24

6 Tompkins Square
9th St. & Ave. A
Saturdays from June 15-November 23

7 St. Marks Church
10th St. and 2nd Ave.
Tuesdays from June 4-December 24

8 West Village
Gansevoort & Hudson Sts.
Saturdays from June 15-November 23

9 Union Square (the best)
17th St. and Broadway
Wednesdays, Fridays and Saturdays, year round

0 East 67th St. *Between 1st and York Aves.*
Saturdays from June 15-December 21

1 West 77th St. & Columbus Ave.
Sundays, year round

2 East 87th St.
Between 1st & 2nd Aves.
Saturdays from June 1-November 23

3 102nd St. & Amsterdam Ave.
Fridays from June 28-December 20

SPECIALIZED GOURMET SHOPS

Labels on map:

W 106 St.
W 96 St.
W 86 St.
W 79 St.
W 72 St.
W 65 St.
W 59 St.
W 57 St.
W 50 St.
W 42 St.
W 34 St.
W 23 St.

E 110 St.
E 106 St.
E 96 St.
E 86 St.
E 79 St.
E 72 St.
E 65 St.
E 59 St.
E 57 St.
E 50 St.
E 42 St.
E 34 St.
E 23 St.
E 14 St.

West End Ave.
Riverside Dr.
Broadway
Amsterdam
Columbus
Central Park West
5 Ave.
Madison
Park
Lexington
3 Ave.
2 Ave.
1 Ave.
York Ave.

CENTRAL PARK

Broadway

11 Ave.
10 Ave.
9 Ave.
8 Ave.
7 Ave.
6 Ave.
5 Ave.
Madison
Park
Lexington
3 Ave.
2 Ave.
1 Ave.
Ave. A

Lincoln Tunnel
Queensborough Br.
Queens - Midtown Tun.
EAST RIVER
FDR Drive

W 14 St.
Greenwich
Hudson
7 Ave. S.
St. Marks Pl.
Bleecker
Houston
Spring
Bowery
Delancey
Williamsburg Br.
Canal
Broadway
East Broadway
Chambers
Manhattan Br.
Fulton
Brooklyn Br.
Wall

HUDSON RIVER
Holland Tunnel
Brooklyn Battery Tunnel

david yeadon ©

1 Bremen House
218 E.86th St. (bet. 2nd & 3rd Aves.)/288-5500
The preeminent German specialist and a real Yorkville mecca. Their meats, cold cuts and imported packaged goods draw a crowd every day. Some elegant gift items, too.

2 Casa Moneo
210 W.14th St. (bet. 7th & 8th Aves.)/929-1644
The prime source for Latino comestibles, many of which are combustibles! If you want to cook a Mexican, Spanish or any other kind of Hispanic dish, you'll find its components here, plus a gift shop upstairs.

3 Caviarteria
29 E.60th St./759-7410, 1-800-221-1020
Only in New York (or maybe Minsk). Their "fish eggs" are of prime quality and their wholesale mail-order trade keeps the counter prices down. If you're not passionate about caviar, check out their other offerings, like smoked salmon and even candy.

4 Cheese of All Nations
153 Chambers St. (off W.Broadway)/732-0752
Literally. We defy you or any cheese gourmand to request one that they don't have on hand. A bonus is the huge cracker selection to go with your choices, if you can squeeze into this cramped space.

5 International Grocery Store
529 9th Ave. (at W.40th St.)/279-5514
Well, it's more Greek Market than anything else but believe us, that's plenty! Bins and barrels of fresh olives, spices and grains beckon (especially one's nose!), and many Middle Eastern delicacies are also available.

Kam Man
200 Canal St. (bet. Mulberry and Mott Sts.)/571-0330
Chinatown's answer to The Bremen House, i.e. an importer-retailer dealing in perishables like marvelous, fresh Oriental veggies, special condiments, spices and exotic jade-work and ivory gifts. Don't neglect their cookware, either.

7 Katagiri
224 E.59th St. (at 3rd Ave.)/755-3566
A Japanese outpost, purveying frozen and fresh entrées, canned and dried items, teas, spices and other bounty from the Land of the Rising Sun. Best to know the basics first.

8 Meyers of Keswick
634 Hudson St. (bet. Horatio and Jane Sts.)/691-4194
The pork pies are better than any you'll find in England. The other meat pies and their Cumberland and Chipolata "bangers" (sausages to American cousins) are unbeatable, too. David Meyers' English shelf items, e.g. the chutneys and mustards, are also first-rate: We just wish it was twice the size.

9 Old Denmark
133 E.65th St. (bet. Lexington and Park Aves.)/744-2533
Take a guess. Right. This one's a Danish den. Their salads, the diverse herring concoctions, patés and spreads, will always be welcome at our smorgasbord! Between 11 and 4 they're a restaurant, too. Stop in for a unique and tasty "tasting" lunch of canapés.

WHOLE FOOD STORES

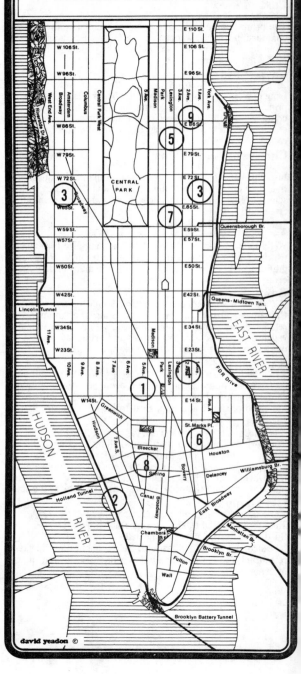

david yeadon ©

1 Brownie's Foods, Inc.
91 5th Ave. (at 16th St.)/242-2199

It opened in 1936, way ahead of its time, and devotees say it still is. The retail operation stocks thousands of organically grown foods, vitamins and specialty items. Alas, their adjoining restaurant once known for its innovative vegetarian cuisine has closed and transmogrified into hip-hop's Union Square Café. What an epitaph!

2 Commodities
117 Hudson St. (at N.Moore St.)/334-8330

They're not kidding. They seem to have the market cornered on every kind of natural food, and the abundance on the shelves is as plentiful as any in a 24-hour superstore. We never knew that there were 125 blends of tea and 50 kinds of honey!

3 Good Earth
182 Amsterdam Ave. (bet. W.68th & W.69th Sts.)/496-1616
1334 1st Ave. (bet. E.71st & E.72nd Sts.)/472-9055
Phone orders delivered

A popular pair, nicely spaced to serve both East & West Siders. Daily offerings at both include hot lunch specials (ziti, tempeh and rice, etc.) and superb soups of the day. . . guaranteed to be savory and filling.

4 Gramercy Natural Foods Center
387 2nd Ave. (bet. E.22nd & E.23rd Sts.)/725-1651

Stop here at lunch and sample one of the sandwiches to go. The herb and spice supply is exceptional, and the produce section, while small, is outstanding.

5 Kubies
1227 Lexington Ave. (at E.83rd St.)/744-3292
Phone orders delivered

Owned and staffed by the Good Earth people, this place also stresses organic bulk foods and unusual concoctions from the kitchen.

6 Pete's Spice Everything Nice Shop
174 1st Ave. (bet. E.10th & E.11th Sts.)/254-8773

Just breathe. . .ahhh! Already you feel better. This aromatic, attractive store features supplies in open bins and gunny sacks, which give it a wonderful, redolent and old-fashioned air. A commendable dried fruit assortment, too.

7 St. Remy
818 Lexington Ave. (off E.62nd St.)/759-8240

Another fragrant floor space. They purvey herbs from their namesake region in France—over 300 varieties in all. The potpourris and soaps make excellent gift items.

8 Whole Foods in SoHo
117 Prince St. (bet. Wooster and Greene Sts.)/673-5388

A gourmet store masquerading as a health food emporium—a whole food half-way house for those who hate the whole notion of "natural living. They allow junk-food diehards to sample the sesame noodles or organic barbequed chicken instead of the Colonel's—that's how converts are won.

9 Yorkville Health Food Center
242 E.86th St. (off 2nd Ave.)/734-6795

This one's a personal favorite, mostly because they're encouraging to unrepentant eaters (like us). They are highly regarded in the industry, too, with kudos for the juice bar, the grain and legume sections, books, and entrepreneurial searches for new sources. The willing and helpful sales force is a blessing that benefits us all.

WINE & SPIRIT SHOPS

david yeadon ©

Acker Merrall & Condit
160 W.72nd St. (bet. Broadway & Columbus Aves.)/787-1700
They opened in 1820 (on another site), which seems to qualify them as the city's oldest, so surely their wines are vintage. Sublime service, too, and their loyal advocacy of house brands is touching.

Astor Wines & Spirits
12 Astor Pl. (at Lafayette St.)/674-7500
The largest libation store in the city, a veritable supermarket of bargains and beverages for shrewd wine lovers. The house labels are dependable and browsing is obligatory.

Cork & Bottle
1158 1st Ave. (bet. E.63rd & E.64th Sts.)/828-5300
The best of the California vineyards are appealingly presented here (and let's not forget that cuttings from our West Coast regenerated France's vineyards after World War II). Prices are more than reasonable.

D. Sokolin
178 Madison Ave. (bet. E.33rd & E.34th Sts.)/532-5893
A university of vintages, a scholarly staff and store publications make this a rather unique establishment. Request your own seminars while you're there for the Thursday night special offerings.

Garnet Liquors
929 Lexington Ave. (bet. E.68th & E.69th Sts.)/772-3211
The "Crazy Eddie" of potable potions, sans manic ad campaign. Peerless prices, strictly cash 'n' carry.

Morrell & Company
535 Madison Ave. (bet. E.54th & E.55th Sts.)/688-9370
Proprietor Peter J. is a forthright, discerning expert and his drinkable stock and reputation always seem to be expanding faster than his new floor space.

Quality House
2 Park Ave. (bet. E.32nd & E.33rd Sts.)/532-2944
It is. Even novices feel comfortable browsing with the best of the oenophiles. And check out that cellar!

Sherry-Lehmann, Inc.
679 Madison Ave. (bet. E.61st & E.62nd Sts.)/838-7500
An old standby among merchants, particularly well-appointed with prize vintages. Frequent sales counterbalance higher prices.

67 Wines and Spirits
179 Columbus Ave. (at E.68th St.)/724-6767
Italian wine lovers will feel especially at home here; French fanciers won't regret a visit either.

SoHo Wines and Spirits
461 W. Broadway (bet. Houston & Prince Sts.)/777-4332
An effervescent shop, very fond of champagne. They'll even help with party planning.

Surrey Liquor Shop
19 E.69th St. (at Madison Ave.)/744-1946
It's about as big or little as the one with the fringe on top too. In other words, this is a small but powerful purveyor. We always enjoy hobnobbing with shrewd staff here: they know their stock and (it seems) everyone else's, too.

ANTIQUE SHOPS

1 A La Vielle Russie
781 5th Ave. (at E.59th St.)/752-1727

No points deducted for mispronouncing their name (Ah la veeay roossie). A unanimous choice, especially for old diamond and emerald pieces, watches and royal knick-knacks from the Czars'era—even an occasional Fabergé egg. Breathtaking.

2 D. Leonard and Gary Trent
Madison Ave (at E.75th St.)/737-9511

We're among the swelling ranks of Tiffany lamp lovers and some of the finest found anywhere are here. Lithographs, silver, bronzes and some nouveau furniture round out the booty of selections.

3 Didier Aaron
32 E.67th St./988-5248

Considered by many to possess one of the best collections of 18th & 19th century European furniture in town, and an ever- changing cluster of old masters. A worthy companion to the Paris original.

4 Garrick C. Stephenson
50 E.57th St./753-2570

A notable reflection of one man's refined—and occasionally amusing — tastes in 18th cent. furniture and decorative arts. Some of the Russian pieces are the epitome of idiosyncrasy.

5 Israel Sack
15 E.57th St./753-6562

Their astonishing assemblage of ancient American furniture and folk art (going back to the Pilgrims) gives them a museum-like air; the wares are priced accordingly. Even their competitors are impressed.

6 Leo Kaplan Antiques
967 Madison Ave. (at E.76th St.)/249-6766

A European cornucopia, and a paperweight fetishist heaven.

7 Lillian Nassau
220 E.57th St. (at 3rd Ave.)/759-6062

Those who die for deco will want to move in. The eager staff's enthusiasm is infectious especially when it comes to the Tiffany collection, so don't be bashful.

8 Philip W. Pfeiffer
900 Madison Ave. (at E.72nd St.)/249-4889

An inspired eccentric regarding inventory. Check out the old time doctors' gear!

9 Stair & Co.
942 Madison Ave. (bet. E.74th & E.75th Sts.)/517-4400

A veddy British firm, headquartered in London. If 18th century English furniture, Chinese porcelains and bits of Victoriana set your heart a-fluttering, look no further. (Don't pass up the **Incurable Collector**, their subsidiary, right across the street.)

0 Urban Archeology
137 Spring St. (at Greene St.)/431-6969

If you consider architectural details (gargoyles, street lamps, cornices, and more) antique, this innovative entrepreneur qualifies. We respect the preservationist spirit and we're fascinated by the artifacts.

*Note: All around 5th Ave. to University Pl. (E.12th-E.9th Sts.) there's a fascinating range of mainly wholesale antique outlets that occasionally offer public sales. Also, while the quality is very variable, **The Manhattan Art & Antiques Center**, 2nd Ave. at E.56th St., 355-4400, is a wonderful 90-store bazaar.*

AUCTION HOUSES

W 106 St.
W 96 St.
W 86 St.
W 79 St.
W 72 St.
W 65 St.
W 59 St.
W 57 St.
W 50 St.
W 42 St.
W 34 St.
W 23 St.
W 14 St.

E 110 St.
E 106 St.
E 96 St.
E 86 St.
E 79 St.
E 72 St.
E 65 St.
E 59 St.
E 57 St.
E 50 St.
E 42 St.
E 34 St.
E 23 St.
E 14 St.

West End Ave.
Amsterdam
Broadway
Columbus
Central Park West
Riverside Dr.
5 Ave.
Madison
Park
Lexington
3 Ave.
2 Ave.
1 Ave.
York Ave.

CENTRAL
PARK

Broadway

11 Ave.
10 Ave.
9 Ave.
8 Ave.
7 Ave.
6 Ave.
5 Ave.
Madison
Park
Lexington
3 Ave.
2 Ave.
1 Ave.
Ave. A

Lincoln Tunnel
Queensborough Br.
Queens - Midtown Tun.
FDR Drive

EAST
RIVER

HUDSON

Greenwich
Hudson
7 Ave. S.
Bleecker
Spring
Canal

St. Marks Pl.
Bowery
Houston
Delancey
Broadway
East Broadway
Williamsburg Br.

RIVER

Holland Tunnel

Chambers
Fulton
Wall

Manhattan Br.
Brooklyn Br.

Brooklyn Battery Tunnel

david yeadon ©

1 Christie's
502 Park Ave. (at E.59th St.)/546-1000

Its London progenitor sets the tone and standards. The finest of fine art, rare manuscripts, exotic tapestries and artifacts highlight the catalogues. The satellite shop is **Christie's East** (219 E.67th St. bet. 2nd & 3rd Aves./606-0400.) for pop items. They've even taken bids on Judy Garland's ruby slippers from "Oz."

2 Greenwich Auction Room
110 E.13th St. (at 4th Ave.)/533-5930

"We do ones no one else has yet conceived," says congenial co-owner Jesse Bien about the Theme Sales often held here. There's "The Fabulous '50s Foray," with a quota of collectibles as well as furniture, and the "Country Fair," with folk art and primitives. Most popular offering is the ad-hoc interior design service which selects from stocked odds and ends to transform your apartment.

3 Lubin Galleries
30 W.26th St. (off 6th Ave.)/924-3777

They handle most of the city's tonier estate auctions, which have a habit of yielding surprises. Few record-breaking prices though, so don't fear.

4 Phillips
406 E.79th St. (at 1st Ave.)/570-4830

This company was founded 20 years after the Declaration of Independence was signed, and many of the paintings they broker are nearly as revered and just as priceless. They usually allow three days exhibition before the strike of the gavel.

5 Sotheby's
1334 York Ave. (at E.72nd St.)/606-7000/7427

By most reckonings, this is the most powerful and influential auctioneer in the world. Record sums are established here, on everything from Rembrandts to the contents of Egyptian pyramids. (Have you priced a sarcophagus lately?) Used as a setting in films and TV shows, an actual visit enables you to observe real-life drama and a poker party of nods and nuances.

6 Tepper Galleries
110 E.25th St. (bet. Park & Lexington Aves.)/677-5300

Estate items and a goodly assortment of baubles, bangles and beads dominate the catalogues here. They've been in business for half a century and have an established reputation as appraisers.

7 William Doyle Galleries
175 E.87th St. (bet. Lexington & 3rd Aves.)/427-2730

Decorative arts from the 16th to 20th centuries are on sale here, alternate Wednesdays, all year round. Because of their knack for snaring the most intriguing estates and consignments, they do the highest volume trading in New York. Twice a year they throw open the doors for a clear-out rummage sale that even duck decoy lovers enjoy.

BICYCLE SHOPS

1 Bicycles Plus
1400 3rd Ave. (bet. E.79th & E.80th Sts.)/794-2929
If you're an East Sider, this a mecca for pedal-power merchandise (to buy or rent). And not only do they do repairs, they have a "beat any price" policy that encourages bargain hunting.

2 Bicycle Renaissance
505 Columbus Ave. (bet. W.84th & W.85th Sts.)/724-2350
This West Side upstart has already earned the respect of its competitors. The "Key Exchange" variety of yuppie has noticed.

3 Broadway Bicycle
663 Amsterdam Ave. (at W.92nd St.)/866-7600
Lots of Central Park riders have discovered this place because they can rent racers reasonably without an F.B.I. investigation.

Brooklyn Bicycle
715 Coney Island Ave. (bet. Ave. C & Cortelyou Rd., Brooklyn)/718-941-9095
It really is worth crossing the river into the land of Flatbush Flashes for fine bike bargains and friendly service here.

4 Conrad's Bike Shop
25 Tudor City Pl. (off E.41st St., near 2nd Ave.)/697-6966
This hi-tech shop caters to pros who compete in grueling cross-country races, but they don't ignore weekend peddlers. (They just charge more!)

5 14th St. Bicycles
332 E.14th St. (bet. 1st & 2nd Aves.)/228-4344
The huge blue and yellow mural has dominated the corner for years, and the shop, one of the city's first (established just in time for the transit strike in '69), is still crazy about bikes after all these years.

6 Frank's Bike Shop
553 Grand St. (at F.D.R. Drive)/533-6332
In addition to a complete inventory of major brands, they carry an invaluable range of hard-to-find accessories, which can also be necessities.

7 Gene's Bicycle Shop
242 E.79th St. (bet. 2nd & 3rd Aves.)/249-9218
The stock brimmeth over, the repairs are highly regarded, the lessons likable and the prices perfect.

8 Pedal Pusher Bike Shop
1306 2nd Ave. (at E.69th St.)/879-0740
We are grateful for their devotion to good ole 3-speeds and old-fashioned codes of customer service.

9 Stuyvesant Bicycle
349 W.14th St. (bet. 8th & 9th Aves.)/254-5200
Many come to ogle at the hi-end and hi-tech dream machines here, the Puchs and Atalas, but their sales volume permits good discounts, and they'll allow a short spin.

FLORISTS

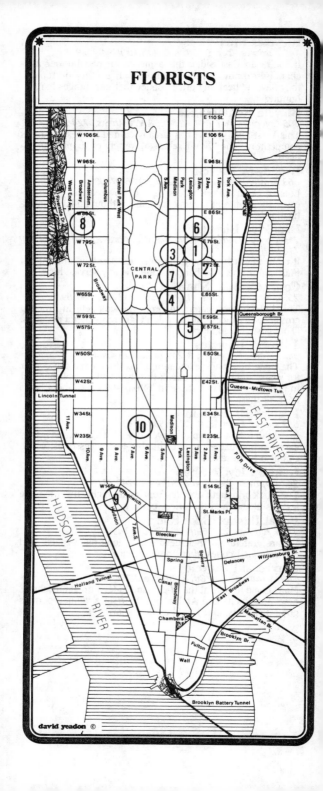

david yeadon ©

1 Bouquets à la Carte
228 E.75th St. (bet. Lexington & 3rd Aves.)/988-3732
Lots of luminaries love their bounteous assortment of fresh and paper flowers. The house specialty is a giant balloon festooned with blossoms and streamers—a great congrats token for special occasions.

2 Ethel Rogers-Fellan Florists
192 E.72nd St. (bet. 2nd & 3rd Aves.)/288-7848
The merger of these two powerhouses has only enhanced their respective reputations. Ethel's custom arrangements remain the most tasteful you can find.

3 Madderlake
25 E.73rd St./879-8400
You'll see plants from all over the world here, California blooms and a vast selection of the exotic. Corporate and other well-heeled party planners keep this place busy. On request you can receive help with other esoterica—like table settings.

4 Renny
27 E.62nd St./371-5354
This is another favorite party source for The Beautiful People. Renny has even been called the Cecil B. deMille of florists, having designed awesome arrangements for celebs. If you stop to listen, you'll hear some eyebrow-raising stories, too.

5 Rialto Florist
707 Lexington Ave. (off E.57th St.)/688-3234
If you ever find yourself working late and almost forgetting that key anniversary, fear not. This excellent full-service shop is open 24 hours a day, 7 days a week.

6 Richard Salome
152 E.79th St. (bet. Lexington & 3rd Aves.)/988-2933
Variety and vivacious displays characterize this uptown charmer catering to a wide range of customer tastes from traditional to super-trendy.

7 Ronaldo Maia Flowers
27 E.67th St. (off 5th Ave.)/288-1049
This Brazilian ex-patriot works wonders with gift baskets and has a striking collection of decorative vases and pots. His 7-scent potpourri is a particular favorite.

8 Surroundings
2295 Broadway (bet. W.82nd & 83rd Sts.)/580-8982
Non-extravagant exercises in creative flower arrangements in lovely containers plus silk flowers and sales people who really seem to enjoy their work.

9 Twigs
399 Bleecker St. (bet. Perry & W.11th Sts.)/620-8188
All very old villagey and perfect for bouquets to make mother smile or for capturing truly romantic hearts. No flash—just fair prices.

10 York Floral
104 W.27th St. (off 6th Ave.)/686-2070
In the heart of the city's flower district, this fragrant, friendly place will sell you all their delightful wares at discount. The rose collection is outstanding, but don't expect uptown frills.

HI-END ELECTRONICS

1 Audio Breakthrough
199 Amsterdam Ave. (bet. W.67th & W.68th St.)/595-7157

Always an excellent selection here, plus some flexibility in prices, especially if an entire system is purchased. Service can be uninterested, especially for novices; the busy salespeople often seem to be responding to some higher authority.

CSA Audio
193 Bellevue Ave./Upper Montclair, NJ/201-744-0600

An exceptional out-of-state mecca loved by NY audiophiles for its full range of the best available equipment, courteous low-key service, leisurely expert advice and ideal "auditioning" environments. Well worth the half hour journey, but avoid Saturdays.

2 Innovative Audio
77 Clinton St./Brooklyn Heights, Brooklyn/718-596-0888/212-619-6400

Another out-of-Manhattan exception, but included for its impressive selection and the pleasant attitude of staff towards extensive equipment testing. Occasionally there's some light-pressure sales, but generally it's relaxed.

3 Lyric Hi-Fi and Video
2005 Broadway (bet. W.73rd & W.74th Sts.)/769-4600
1221 Lexington Ave. (off E.79th St.)/535-5710

Top equipment with prices to match, featuring the latest and most fashionable appliances. The average customer should know that unless he's definitely dropping a bundle, he may get short shrift from staff.

4 Sound by Singer
165 E.33rd St. (bet. 3rd & Lexington Aves.)/683-0925

A carefully selected range of some of the best equipment available, but customers get the impression that they must acknowledge the owner's self-proclaimed omniscience in matters electronic if they want to join the "quality clientele" club.

5 Stereo Exchange
687 Broadway (bet. E.3rd & E.4th Sts.)/505-1111

While carrying a full complement of audiophile components, the store deals primarily in hi-end used equipment. If you know what you want, excellent bargains can be had and trade-ins are accepted—but don't expect too much from the staff other than encouragement to purchase promptly.

HOUSEWARES AND HARDWARE

W 106 St.
W 96 St.
W 86 St.
W 79 St.
W 72 St.
W 65 St.
W 59 St.
W 57 St.
W 50 St.
W 42 St.
W 34 St.
W 23 St.
W 14 St.

Riverside Dr.
West End Ave.
Broadway
Amsterdam
Columbus
Central Park West
Broadway
11 Ave.
10 Ave.
9 Ave.
8 Ave.
7 Ave.
6 Ave.
5 Ave.
7 Ave. S.
Greenwich
Hudson

E 110 St.
E 106 St.
E 96 St.
E 86 St.
E 79 St.
E 72 St.
E 65 St.
E 59 St.
E 57 St.
E 50 St.
E 42 St.
E 34 St.
E 23 St.
E 14 St.

5 Ave.
Madison
Park
Lexington
3 Ave.
2 Ave.
1 Ave.
York Ave.
Ave. A

CENTRAL
PARK

Queensborough Br.
Queens - Midtown Tun.
Lincoln Tunnel

EAST RIVER
FDR Drive

HUDSON
RIVER

Holland Tunnel

St. Marks Pl.
Bleecker
Houston
Spring
Delancey
Williamsburg Br.
Canal
Broadway
Bowery
East Broadway
Chambers
Manhattan Br.
Fulton
Brooklyn Br.
Wall

Brooklyn Battery Tunnel

david yeadon ©

Note:If you really want to have fun seeking out hard-to-find hard-ware, check the bazaar along Canal St. (bet. W.Broadway and Lafayette St.)

Bridge Kitchenware
214 E.52nd St. (bet. 2nd & 3rd Aves.)/688-4220
Competitors won't be countenanced here. They claim to be the best, and well they might be, especially if you measure the inventory. It's all here, including industrial strength appliances and a knife collection a cut above the rest.

Brookstone
18 Fulton St. (at The South Street Seaport)/344-8108
1 Herald Square at Herald Center (W.34th St. & Broadway)/564-7661
The New Hampshire legend, laden with esoteric tools and gadgets and using a unique hi-tech sales system. You'll buy things here you never knew existed, and the staff is happy to consult with you on usage, should you need their services. If you can't come yourself, they'll send you a mail order catalogue, but then you'll miss out on all the fun. Also, while you're at the South Street Seaport visit **The Sharper Image** at Pier 17 for unusual and amusing household items.

Conran's
2-8 Astor Place (at Broadway)/505-1515
160 E.54th St. (in the Citicorp Center)/371-2225
Contemporary and clean, comfortable for browsing, and the prices are compatible. They're strong on hi-tech and hi-fashion household items (almost all imported from England)—everything from towel racks and knobs to yards and yards of fabrics and matching wallpapers, modular furniture and innovative doodads that spice up the abode and zing it with primary and pastel colors. The staff looks as fresh and clean as the merchandise.

D.F. Saunders
386 W. Broadway (bet. Spring & Broome Sts.)/925-9040
952 Madison Ave. (bet. E.74th & E.75th Sts.)/879-6161
There are lots of heavy-duty industrial appliances here (a vacuum cleaner that really gets the dirt out because it knows how to suck it all up—with 3.5 horsepower) and plenty of hardware for making repairs.

Hoffritz
331 Madison Ave. (at E.43rd St.)/697-7344
The hi-priced housewares and cutlery shop in town with a full line of imported goodies, especially blades, to choose from, and other advanced adult toys for people who have everything. There's more even at **Hammacher Schlemmer** at 147 E.57th St./421-9000, where the stuff gets really sophisticated; including silent butlers that press pants, tabletop corkpullers, and unimaginable devices for doing things you never knew needed doing.

Manhattan Ad-Hoc
842 Lexington Ave. (at E.64th St.)/752-5488
The entire floor radiates a quirky spontaneous charm, with sparkling glassware in all shapes and sizes. An aptly named conglomeration of trifles and other kitchen and household necessaries for serving in style.

The Pottery Barn
117 E.59th St/753-5424 and many other locations
Popular with the proletariat and peasants among us, as well as the yuppies. They have the largest selection of mugs, jugs, flowerpots, dishes, glassware and fine porcelain at close-out and warehouses prices.

JEWELRY SHOPS

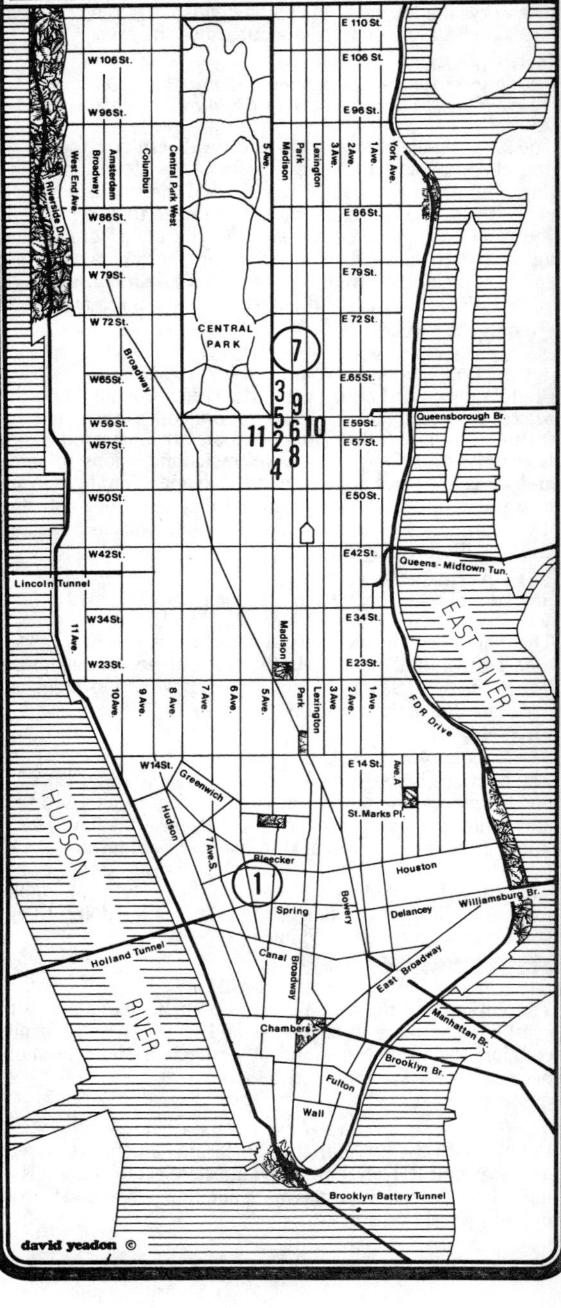

W 110 St.   E 110 St.
W 106 St.   E 106 St.
W 96 St.   E 96 St.
W 86 St.   E 86 St.
W 79 St.   E 79 St.
W 72 St.   E 72 St.

CENTRAL PARK

W 65 St.   E 65 St.
W 59 St.   E 59 St.
W 57 St.   E 57 St.
W 50 St.   E 50 St.
W 42 St.   E 42 St.
W 34 St.   E 34 St.
W 23 St.   E 23 St.

Riverside Dr.
West End Ave.
Amsterdam
Broadway
Columbus
Central Park West
5 Ave.
Madison
Park
Lexington
3 Ave.
2 Ave.
1 Ave.
York Ave.

Queensborough Br.

7
3 9 10
5 6
11 2 8
4

Lincoln Tunnel

Queens - Midtown Tun.

EAST RIVER

FDR Drive

11 Ave.
10 Ave.
9 Ave.
8 Ave.
7 Ave.
6 Ave.
5 Ave.
Madison
Park
Lexington
3 Ave.
2 Ave.
1 Ave.
Ave. A

HUDSON

W 14 St.   E 14 St.
Greenwich   St. Marks Pl.
Hudson
7 Ave. S.
Bleecker   Houston
Bowery
1
Spring   Delancey   Williamsburg Br.

Holland Tunnel

Canal
Broadway
East Broadway

RIVER

Chambers

Manhattan Br.

Brooklyn Br.

Fulton

Wall

Brooklyn Battery Tunnel

david yeadon ©

1 Artwear
456 W.Broadway (at Prince St.)/673-2000/3388
Art is what you'll wear, all right. This is also possibly listed among the major SoHo galleries for its masterworks. Owner-artist Robert Lee Morris delights in displaying the work of many jewelers here and at his second gallery at 409 W.Broadway.

2 Buccellati
Trump Tower/725 5th Ave./308-5533
46 E. 57th St./308-2900
Gold & Silver Milan style (which needs to be seen to be defined) in the rarified atmosphere of Donald's pink and gold fantasy.

3 Bulgari
Hotel Pierre/2 E.61st St./486-0086
A confining space with a world-wide reach. Gem stones in custom settings are the specialty.

4 Cartier
653 5th Ave. (at E.52nd St.)/753-0111 and other locations
Their "les must" are a must. This contemporary jeweler with old fashioned reputation offers eclectic gifts and doesn't discourage down-market browsers who know how to go prospecting and strike gold.

5 David Webb
7 E.57th St. (off 5th Ave.)/421-3030
Memories of his animal collection linger and his gold creations are copied by everyone. Very popular.

6 F. Staal
5 E.57th St. (off 5th Ave.)/758-1821
A tiny establishment renown for all the old-fashioned values of fine worksmanship, excellent quality and unsurpassed service for connoisseurs of top-drawer estate jewelry.

7 Fred Leighton
781 Madison Ave. (at E.66th St.)/288-1872
A remarkably genial concern where Murray Leighton proudly displays his collection of outstanding antique jewelry and has become the master of tasteful, personal service. Also don't miss **Veronique Cartier's** fabulous modern creations here.

8 Harry Winston
718 5th Ave. (at W.56th St.)/245-2000
The premier American diamond house. Classics, orthodox and up-to-date settings are available here at the Grand Salon with top quality stones at the right price, and you'll still be treated like royalty. (The Petit Salon can be found at Trump Tower.)

9 James Robinson
15. E.57th St./752-6166
Wonderful range of antique pieces from just about everywhere that was anywhere.

10 Tiffany & Co.
727 5th Ave. (at E.57th St.)/755-8000
Both rarified and approachable at once, its reputation precedes it. A cornucopia of glorious gold, silver and gems, crystals and porcelains. . .party time for a princess, wrapped in the sky blue box.

11 Van Cleef & Arpels
744 5th Ave. (at 57th St.)/644-9500
Elegant and somehow understated, too. The design tradition goes back to adorning 19th century monarchs. For Christmas they bring out Empress Josephine's tiara.

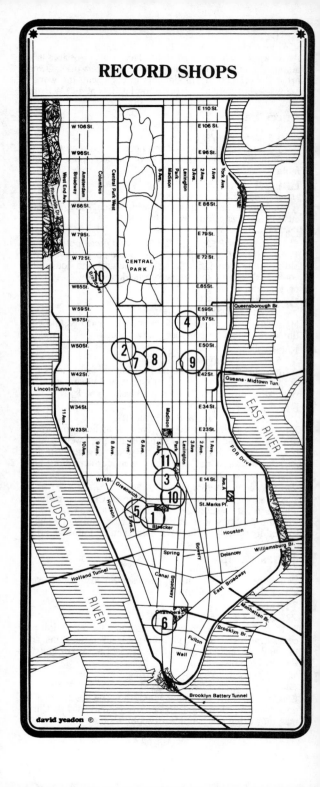

RECORD SHOPS

1 Bleecker Bob's Golden Oldies
118 W.3rd St. (bet. 6th Ave. & MacDougal St.)/475-9677
Yeah, yeah, yeah, there's jukebox jewelry here, especially British issue. Plenty of New Wave, too, as the address implies.

2 Colony Records
1619 Broadway (at W.49th St.)/265-2050
A dependable veteran since Tin Pan Alley days, with all that's new and plenty that's not. Need a tracer on a wax or vinyl fossil? Call 'em.

3 Dayton's
824 Broadway (at E.12th St.)/254-5084
Soundtrack City, plus plenty of reviewer's copies in mint condition at half-price.

4 Discomat
716 Lexington Ave. (at E.57th St)/759-3777 also at many other locations
Appealing prices, presumably aided by their cash-only policy. All the top 40's, rock, jazz, and reggae are here. Hardly a haven for classical fans.

5 The Golden Disc
239 Bleecker St. (at 6th Ave.)/255-7899
The malt shop of record stores, specializing in every 45 oldie you ever played on a quarter.

6 J & R Music World
23 Park Row (off Broadway)/732-8600 and many other locations
Their inventory, which runs the gamut from pop to Pavarotti (and everything between) is as extensive as the listings on the big board of the neighboring stock exchange. They sell stereo equipment at good prices too.

7 Music Masters
25 W.43rd St. (off 6th Ave.)/840-1958
One for the opera fans, where you can listen before you buy. Lot's of theatre and classical music here, too.

8 The Record Hunter
507 5th Ave. (at E.43rd St.)/697-8970
There are plenty of contraltos, bassos, et al here, too, along with a full line of most other idioms, including country. Interestingly, their stock is thinnest in the rock pile.

9 Sam Goody
66 3rd Ave (at E.43rd St.)/986-8480 and many other locations
For our money, they're the best mass marketers of discs and reels. Don't expect to find rarities here. Watch for frequent sales.

10 Tower Records
Broadway (at W.66th St.)/799-2500
Broadway (at W.4th St.)/505-1500
The ultimate Manhattan sound emporium, with a virtually inexhaustable inventory and their own newspaper. Their glitzy neon decor is a bonus and it's a great way to browse for more than just records on a rainy afternoon—especially the NoHo branch on W.4th St.

11 The Wiz
E.14th St. at Union Square/741-9500 and many other locations
For soul, rhythm & blues, dance music BLS, KISS, QHT and club style, their inventory can't be beat, plus they have all the other stuff at discount. Weak on the classical side, but then, they do have "standards." Electronics available here at discount, too.

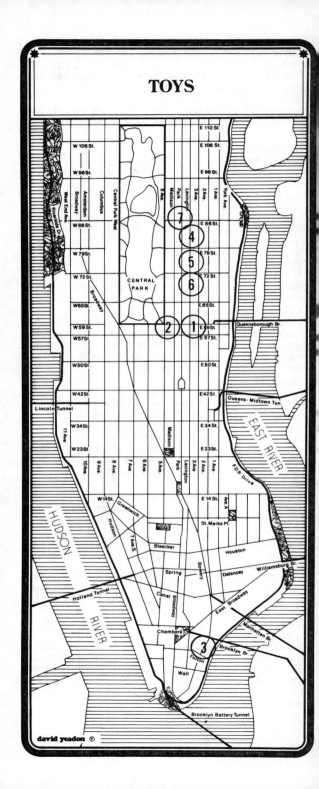

TOYS

1 Childcraft Center
150 E.58th St. (bet. Lexington & 3rd Aves.)/753-3196

Their wooden blocks and other hard-to-break offerings are the stock-in-trade of this innovative outfit. If there's a budding engineer in your family, he or she will love the construction kits. These, plus other educational items—science projects, musical instruments and more, prove that toys really teach too.

2 F.A.O. Schwarz
A recent relocation to The General Motors Building on E.58th and Madison (with another entrance at E.58th St. and 5th Ave.)/644-9400 (also at the World Trade Center and other locations)

The biggest stuffed animals in captivity fill their floors, plus toy cars that kids can drive, and trains on tracks that carry passengers, wagons, bikes and imports of the most extravagant toys in the world. This famous fantasy-parlor is a visual feast year-round and the Christmas season is the absolute best. But if you want something special, be sure you stop at the bank first.

3 Geppetto's Toys
205 Front St. (at The South Street Seaport)/608-1239

As you might suspect, they sell marionettes, although none have come to life so far. Parents and grandparents who remember their favorite playthings will want to visit this throwback; it's filled with nonelectronic, no-batteries-necessary amusements. (Applause, applause.)

4 Go Fly a Kite
1201 Lexington Ave. (bet. E.81st & E.82nd St.)/472-2623

By all means if you stop here, 'specially on a warm April afternoon when the breezes are favorable and there isn't a cloud in the sky, you won't be able to restrain yourself. A true original and a personal favorite.

5 Laughing Giraffe
1065 Lexington Ave. (bet. E.75th & E.76th Sts.)/570-9528

And why shouldn't he? This trim shop is owned and operated by ex-teachers who obviously care about the quality of children's fun. Bravo for their book section, and for the credo that merriment can be enriching.

6 Mary Arnold Toys
962 Lexington Ave. (at E.70th St.)/744-8510

Recently remodeled, this remains a kingdom for cuddly bears and such, along with extras like art supplies and helium balloons. There are some nice dollhouses, too. Their clever sales gimmick of inviting kids to write "wish lists" can be combustible, though.

7 Toy Park
112 E.86th St. (bet. Park & Lexington Aves.)/427-6611

Well-named; it's about as big as a city common, and a veritable supermarket/department store—the stuff of kid's dreams. If you can't find it here, give up! We're particularly impressed with their dolls and games inventory.

UNUSUAL BOOKSHOPS

david yeadon ©

1 Argosy
116 E.59th St. (bet. Park & Lexington Aves.)/753-4455
Whoever coined that old saw about being doomed to repeat mistakes unless we study history would applaud this retrospective specialist. European and American chronicles are the stock-in-trade, along with an outstanding biography collection.

2 The Complete Traveller
199 Madison Ave. (at E.35th St.)/679-4339/685-9007
Full or part-time sojourners, or those who simply like to dream of faraway places can journey anywhere in almost any era via a leisurely browse through these well-stocked stacks.

3 Eeyore's
2252 Broadway (bet. W.78th & W.79th St.)/362-0634
1066 Madison Ave. (off E.81st St.)/988-3404
During a time when childhood innocence seems to have been revoked by decree, we salute this purveyor of kiddie lit. Classics and the best of the new co-exist triumphantly in both shops, plus those Sunday morning stories (call for details).

4 Gotham Book Mart
41 W.47th St./719-4448
A Diamond District gem with a thousand literary facets and an almost tangible literati tradition. Still sparkles.

5 Kitchen Arts & Letters
1435 Lexington Ave. (bet. E.93rd & E.94th Sts.)/876-5550
A cook's delight! Every conceivable cook book, including many out-of-print, covering every country, cuisine and culinary persuasion. Antique menus and kitchen art, too. Easy to love, hard to leave.

6 Murder Ink
271 W.87th St. (bet. Amsterdam & Columbus Aves.)/362-8905
Detective fiction's recent resurgence of respectability is reflected in this merchant's growth in floor space and repute. Along with **The Mysterious Bookshop** at 129 W.56th St./759-0900, they serve fans of the genre with faithfulness and charm.

7 The Traveller's Bookstore
22 W.52nd St. (off 5th Ave.)/664-0995
An invaluable resource for restless spirits. This 5-year-old niche is hidden in the lobby of the Warner Building, offering a vast selection of U.S. and foreign published travel books and maps, including their own catalogue, and lots of free, reliable advice.

8 Sam Weiser's Books
132 E.24th St. (bet. Park Ave. So. & Lexington Ave.)/777-6363
Bewitching source for metaphysical and occult topics complete with crystal balls, tarot cards and voodoo dolls. Most diverting!

Strand Bookstore *see UNUSUAL STORES I*

Union Theological Seminary Bookstore
3401 Broadway (at W.120th St.)/662-7100
The **Gotham Book Mart's** famous "Wise Men Fish Here" sign would be appropriate hanging here. Maintained primarily for students, their abundant source of religious writings is available to all souls. A rather more esoteric range can be found at **East-West Books** on 5th Ave. and 13th St./243-5994

UNUSUAL SHOPS I

1 Casswell-Massey
518 Lexington Ave. (at E.48th St.)/755-2254
This legendary partnership was formed in the days when pharmacies were apothecaries and druggists were chemists. The genealogy dates back to George Washington and Cologne No.6, which they still sell. Such history and gentility continue to pervade the place and their artistic catalogue. Cucumber cream, anyone?

2 Chick Darrow's Fun Antiques
E.61st St. at 2nd Ave./838-0730
Wind-up toys, piggy banks, Hollywood bric-a-brac, all sorts of glorious junque fill this space like an enchanted attic crammed with childhood memorabilia. Collectibles abound.

3 Dollhouse Antics
1308 Madison Ave. (bet. E.92nd & E.93rd Sts.)/876-2288
The closest we've ever come to feeling like Gulliver was when we entered this Lilliputianesque realm. The finished miniature homes have literally everything but the plumbing. You can also choose kits to assemble to your own taste. No exaggeration—you can buy a small-scale version of anything you'd purchase for a real house, including occupants.

4 Forbidden Planet
821 Broadway (at E.12th St.)/473-1576
Fans of science fiction are transported to other worlds here. In addition to editions of virtually every book and comic in this overlooked and often mistakenly dismissed genre, the floor space is evocatively accented with aliens and heros from the literature, fantasy art and other amazing fantasmagorical stuff. Shoplifters will be disintegrated, says management.

5 Gallery of Wearable Art
480 W.Broadway (at Houston St.)/425-5379
If you wish to make a personal statement with your fashions, this is your source for hand-painted and handmade creations from 6 continents and 1000 designers. Considered to be the most romantic clothing store in town. Lovers love it, with its Paris art nouveau decor, softly glowing pink interior and a comfortable lounge for men-in-waiting. Female executives be advised: if you conform to office and boardroom dress codes, this place is not for you.

6 Rita Ford, Inc.
19 E.65th St./535-6717
Is there anyone who hasn't been delighted or soothed by a music box at least once? The demand on inventory here indicates that the definitive answer is "no." There's every conceivable kind, from ornate to prim, old to new. You needn't buy to be charmed; simply stop, look and listen.

7 Soldier Shop
1222 Madison Ave. (at E.88th St.)/535-6788
Military mavens are in hog heaven here. Books, toy troops, tin soldiers, medals, battle ribbons, and assorted spoils of war on display. Cue the Patton March.

8 Strand Bookstore
828 Broadway (at E.12th St.)/473-1452
A bibliophile's and bargain-seeker's paradise with over 8 miles of books at amazing discounts and the fantastic 'underground' offering even cheaper selections and a special room for rare volumes. A treasured city institution.

UNUSUAL SHOPS II

david yeadon ©

1 Ace Banner & Flag Co.
107 W.27th St. (at 6th Ave.)/620-9111

Maker of the biggest, smallest, most diverse flags imaginable, including every national banner on earth. If you're pondering a political power-play, the customized pins, patches and pens (not to mention balloons, buttons and bumperstickers) are just the ticket.

2 Back Date Magazines (A&S Book Company)
274 W.43rd St. (bet. 7th & 8th Ave.)/695-4897

Every periodical you ever tossed in the trash has found its way here, but you'll have to pay more than the old newsstand price if you want to retrieve a copy or two.

3 The Camp Shop
41 W.54th St./505-0980

For generations this mother's helper has been sticking the names on clothes for sleepaway and day campers of all shapes and sizes for free. Uniforms are purveyed here as if they were Parisian imports. Duffles, knapsacks, backpacks. . .if you need it, they have it.

4 Gordon Novelty Co.
933 Broadway (bet. W. 21st & W.22nd Sts.)/254-8616

Evocative of Halloween, even in April, and therefore it can't be bad at all. In fact it's heart winning, mostly for the gags that used to be sold in the comic books. Fellow fans of masks, costumes and such stuff will lose track of time here.

5 James Lowe Autographs
30 E.60th St./Suite 907/759-0775

A palpable sense of history here pervades the atmosphere and transports you through a time-warp. The letters, signatures, photographs and doodles of Napoleon, Beethoven and Gandhi are goosebump generators, not to mention history's other major mentionables, who are well-represented.

6 Mabel's
849 Madison Ave.(bet. E.70th & E.71st Sts.)/734-3263

A lady called Peaches who'd name her place for her cat must keep an interesting shop and she does. Gifts for animal lovers abound here, as do all manner of one-of-a-kind doodads.

7 Mythology Unlimited
370 Columbus Ave. (bet. W.77th & 78th Sts.)/874-0774

A chameleon of a store; it seems to change with every vibration in pop culture. If it's trendy, attention-getting or just plain odd, you'll find it here. Check out gumball machines, masks, godzillas, even build-it-yourself Statues of Liberty.

8 Only Hearts   *12-7 Sun*
281 Columbus Ave. (bet. W.68th & W.69th Sts.)/724-5608

Cupid must be their major stockholder; everything is shaped like or decorated with hearts. Shop early for St. Valentine's Day. *386 Columbus   So. of 79th*

9 Serendipity 3   *across from Museum of Natural History*
225 E.60th St. (bet. 2nd & 3rd Aves.)/838-3531

The only gift shop we know of that doubles as an ice cream parlor, and is therefore a favorite with kids. Cleverly executed and cute. If this kind of thing appeals, visit **Agora** (1550 3rd Ave. at E.78th St.) for a mix of ice cream parlor; soda-counter and boutique.

10 Steuben Glass
56th St. and 5th Ave./752-1441

A fabulous store/gallery for superb crystal creations, all with that unmistakable Steuben flair.

CHILDREN'S FASHIONS

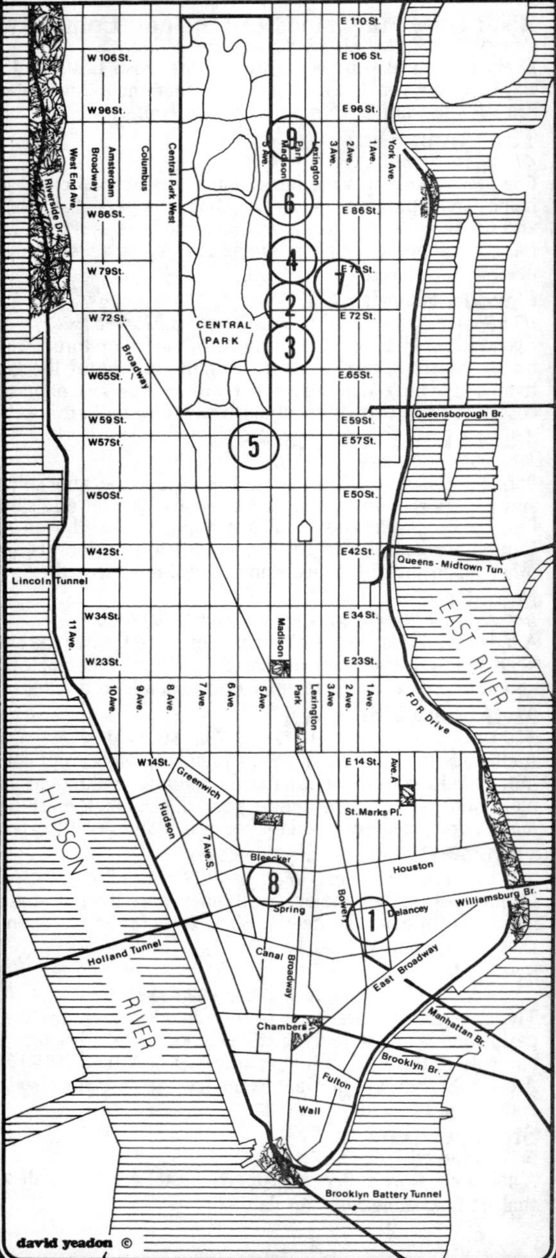

Map labels (Manhattan):

W 106 St. · W 96 St. · W 86 St. · W 79 St. · W 72 St. · W 65 St. · W 59 St. · W 57 St. · W 50 St. · W 42 St. · W 34 St. · W 23 St. · W 14 St.

E 110 St. · E 106 St. · E 96 St. · E 86 St. · E 79 St. · E 72 St. · E 65 St. · E 59 St. · E 57 St. · E 50 St. · E 42 St. · E 34 St. · E 23 St. · E 14 St.

West End Ave. · Riverside Dr. · Amsterdam · Broadway · Columbus · Central Park West · Central Park · 5 Ave. · Madison · Park · Lexington · 3 Ave. · 2 Ave. · 1 Ave. · York Ave.

11 Ave. · 10 Ave. · 9 Ave. · 8 Ave. · 7 Ave. · 6 Ave. · 5 Ave. · Park · Lexington · 3 Ave. · 2 Ave. · 1 Ave. · Ave. A · F.D.R. Drive

Lincoln Tunnel · Holland Tunnel · Queensborough Br. · Queens - Midtown Tun. · Williamsburg Br. · Manhattan Br. · Brooklyn Br. · Brooklyn Battery Tunnel

Greenwich · Hudson · 7 Ave. S. · Bleecker · Spring · Canal · Broadway · Bowery · East Broadway · Delancey · Houston · St. Marks Pl. · Chambers · Fulton · Wall

HUDSON RIVER · EAST RIVER

Circled numbers: 9, 6, 4, 1, 2, 3, 5, 8, 1

david yeadon ©

Note: Children's clothes can be prohibitively expensive, and it's often best to check discounters first, instead of the department stores, for real bargains. Remember, kids grow fast. (The best basement bargains for babies are in Boro Park, Brooklyn, but that's another story.)

1 A&G Infants & Children's Wear
261 Broome St. (off Orchard St.)/966-3775
Ask any stroller-pusher in the neighborhood, and they'll vouch for this enterprise which specializes in name brands at discount. A resource worth having.

2 Au Chat Botte
903 Madison Ave. (bet. E.72nd & E.73rd Sts.)/772-7402
Beautiful baby boutique. You'll find French, Italian, British and other European wares here, plus shoes.

3 Cerutti
807 Madison Ave. (bet. E.67th & E.68th Sts.)/737-7540
One of their competitors said admiringly, "They're the mother of us all." And indeed their mix of domestic and imported garments is impressive for both quality and price. Casual and formal styles peacefully co-exist on well-stocked racks.

4 Glad Rags
1007 Madison Ave. (at E.78th St.)/988-1880
And you thought only advertising was dispensed on this boulevard! Their underwear to outerwear line reaches from the cradle to size 18.

5 Kidz at Bendel
10 W.57th St./247-1100
A trendy little department, featuring all natural fiber clothes, with clever educational toys thrown in for good measure.

6 Little Bits
1186 Madison Ave. (bet. E.86th & E.87th Sts.)/722-6139
This unique shop is a family affair: mother and daughter advertise and market father's designs. Much of the merchandise is handmade, and contrary to what that normally implies, the prices are never inflated.

7 Peter Elliot's Whimsey
1335 3rd Ave. (bet. E.76th & E.77th St.)/861-4200
Your children won't pout here. It's almost an F.A.O. Schwarz, with all the stuffed animals and other colorful temptations. (Does anyone have a gag for the brat who always screams, "Buy it, I want it now!"?). Yes, they have plenty of togs, too, from all the latest designers of children's wear, like Lilac Bush, Jean Le Bourget and New Man.

8 Wendy's
131 Wooster St. (bet. Prince & Houston Sts.)/533-2306
A well-stocked, expertly managed outpost in SoHo, and what with the gentrifying middle classes and their burgeoning families, boy do they need it.

9 Wicker Gardens Baby
1327 Madison Ave. (bet. E.93rd & E.94th Sts.)/348-1166
The source for exquisite infant and toddler wraps, including custom-made christening outfits. **The Children's Wing**, adjoining at 1325 Madison Ave. (410-7001), is equally fine for school-age youngsters.

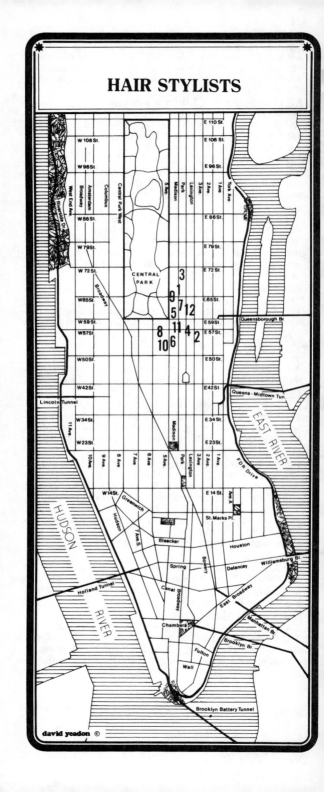

HAIR STYLISTS

david yeadon ©

1 Bruno Dessange
760 Madison Ave. (bet. E.65th & E.66th Sts.)/517-9660
A light-hearted Gallic atmosphere prevails, as everyone here speaks French. These stylists can be original, but will cut to the contours of the individual face.

2 Bumble and Bumble
146 E.56th St. (bet. Lexington & 3rd Aves.)/371-4100
Hi-tech, innovative, but no-nonsense, with decor and staff contributing to a fun-charged atmosphere. They welcome your input on what flatters you most.

3 Davir
30 E.67th St. (off Madison Ave.)/249-3550
An elegant Continental salon featuring French stylists who know color correction, streaking and styling better than most. Some complaints, recently, though.

4 Gerard Bollei
115 E.57th St. (bet. Park & Lexington Aves.)/759-7985
Innovators in hair fashions for high fashion looks. This is where the fash-mags come to find out what's 'in' next season. Such sumptuous interiors that a major design magazine gave them a full feature.

5 Gio
Pierre Hotel/2 E.61st St./308-7600
The inimitable Gio Hernandez goes on forever in this male superstar oasis, where high-flying clients relax in the marble and mirrored setting before receiving perfect perms and pedicures.

6 Kenneth
19 E.54th St. (off 5th Ave.)/752-1800
Preeminent city stylist, specializing in intricate constructions, not simple cuts. For the older generation of socialite. ("Height, darling, I need height!")

7 La Coupe
694 Madison Ave. (at E.62nd St.)/371-9230
Hot, unisex, packed out, popular and versatile. La Coupe even puts out its own distinguished line of hair-care products.

8 Le Salon
16 W.57th St. (bet. 5th and 6th Aves.)/581-2760
The "Natural Look" prevails here, as decreed by Bruno, the Italian designer. The clientele swear by the easy-to-care-for results. Color corrections and tinting are popular, too.

9 Monsieur Marc
22 E.65th St. (off 5th Ave.)/861-0700
Nancy Reagan goes here, and so do others caught in a time warp. No blow dryers.

10 Pipino-Buccheri
14 E.55th St. (off 5th Ave., 2nd floor)/759-2959
Full service salon, catering to easy-care contemporary looks that make you look better walking out than you did walking in; quite an accomplishment in these days of freaky-do's.

11 Suga
115 E.57th St. (bet. Park & Lexington Aves.)/421-4400
This Japanese stylist is considered the best, bar none. Full service salon offers everything in hair care, and the staff is Suga trained. Plan well in advance for an appointment.

Xavier
692 Madison Ave. (bet. E.62nd & E.63rd Sts.)/751-8588
The natural look reigns here—classic, easy-to-care-for cuts, highlights that last and hair-dos that don't tangle. Accomodating appointments policy for busy folks.

MEN'S DISCOUNT FASHIONS

1 BFO and BFO Plus
149 5th Ave. (at 21st St.)/254-0059

If your pride smarts because you must shop for discounts (which we think is silly, 'cause it's how the rich stay that way), this haberdashery, frequented by moneybags and others, is for you.

2 Dollar Bill's
E. 42nd St. and Park Ave. (in Grand Central Terminal)/867-0212

In addition to the hi-fashion women's designer imports, this unlikely location (it used to be a Rexall Pharmacy and then a 69¢ store) has capitalized on its convenience, and offers a full line of menswear and accessories, as well as odd-lotted housewares and tobacco products at super-reduced prices.

3 Eisenberg & Eisenberg
85 5th Ave. (at E.16th St., 2nd floor)/627-1296

Part of the 5th Ave. discount market offering factory prices for top-line names.

4 Harry Rothman
200 Park Ave. So. (at E.17th St.)/777-7400

Harry and his brother Jack should be commended for their perserverance (they've been around for decades) and their commitment to 50% markdowns plus a decent selection of hard-to-find Big & Tall sizes and other hard-to-fit consumers. The range and quality of outerwear is impressive.

5 Hertling & Pollack
85 5th Ave. (bet. 15th & 16th Sts.)/242-4412/243-2420

Top quality merchandise at bargain basement prices. You'll be surprised.

6 L&S Men's Clothing
23 W.45th St. (bet. 5th & 6th Aves.)/575-0933

This is where business executives with acute sense of style and dollops of frugality shop for their Hickey-Freeman's and other designer duds at up to 65% off.

7 Merns Mart
75 Church St. (across from the World Trade Center)

Seemingly endless selection of American, French and British creations for both sexes, with hefty discounts (and shoes, too!).

8 Moe Ginsburg
162 5th Ave. (at E.21st St., 7th floor)/982-5254

Another component of the 5th Ave. discount group, with a vast choice of designer wear at good (but not always outstanding) discounts. So haggle a little. . .

9 NBO
1965 Broadway (at W.67th St.)/595-1550 and other locations

Known for carrying everything except the shoes, this famous discounter does well in representing the current European and American fashions at considerable discount.

Syms *see WOMEN'S DISCOUNT FASHIONS*

MEN'S HIGH FASHIONS

david yeadon ©

Note: As much as we admire Bijan and other designer enclaves, we have selected stores open to everyone on a regular basis. Many also have excellent women's fashion departments.

1 Alfred Dunhill
620 5th Ave. (at 50th St.)/489-5580

Splendid selection of sweaters, blazers, tailored suits, plus sportswear and all those elite accessories. For the even more discriminating, there's custom menswear at **Dunhill Tailors** at 65 E.57th St./355-0050.

2 Barney's
W.17th St. and 7th Ave./929-9000

They lay claim to being the largest haberdashery in the world, and they just might be. They've got tens of thousands of suits in inventory, plus barbershop, a bar and a gift shop, as well as a women's boutique. They also used to be a lot less expensive so now it pays to wait for the sales and get there real early.

3 Brooks Brothers
346 Madison Ave. (at E.44th St.)/682-8800

Classic is not stodgy, and for what seems like centuries these haberdashers have proved it with dash. They are a national institution and half of the older traders on Wall Street would walk around naked without them. Plus ça change, plus c'est la même chose.

4 Charivari
2339 Broadway (at W.85th St.)/873-7242 and others

This is a fortress of high fashion, one of the few outside the department stores, where you can get your hands on the latest looks prescribed by Hollywood and other image-makers. Caters to a younger group and proves it with its fast-pace, hi-volume music and contemporary displays. All the major leagues are repped, including **Giorgio Armani** (own store at 650 5th Ave. at E.68th St./265-2760) and **Gianni Versace**, (816 Madison Ave.at E.52nd St./744-5572.) Other stores have a broader selection of styles for both sexes.

5 Ferragamo Uomo
730 5th Ave. (bet. E.56th & E.57th Sts.)/246-6211

There's more to Ferragamo than the widely known stock of handmade shoes, which have impeccable reputation. The clothes are a contemporary classic line made from the finest Italian fabrics with the same attention to quality and detail as the footgear.

6 Paul Stuart
Madison Ave. at E.45th St./682-0320

A wide selection of top-quality suits, shirts and ties, slacks and sportcoats, all exquisitely-tailored for the boardroom look. Don't leave home without "it", 'cause sales here are rare and discounts don't exist.

7 Ralph Lauren/Polo
867 Madison Ave. (at E.72nd St.)/606-2100

Ralph always does it in style, ensconced in the Rhinelander Mansion, from denims to dinner jackets. The clubby atmosphere and amenities on the sales floor are further proof of his good taste, and even his prices are reasonable for both sexes.

Saint Laurent, Rive Gauche
534 Madison Ave. (at E.55th St.)/371-7912

Just as classic in menswear as he is in womenswear. He translates his clean lines in a variety of sumptuous fabrics, all of them created to endure. No disposable suits here.

WOMEN'S DISCOUNT FASHIONS

Central Park

Central Park West

Riverside Dr.

West End Ave.

Broadway

Amsterdam

Columbus

5 Ave.

Madison

Lexington

3 Ave.

2 Ave.

1 Ave.

York Ave.

W 106 St. — E 110 St.
W 96 St. — E 106 St.
— E 96 St.
W 86 St. — E 86 St.
W 79 St. — E 79 St.
W 72 St. — E 72 St.
W 65 St. — E 65 St.
W 59 St. — E 59 St.
W 57 St. — E 57 St.
W 50 St. — E 50 St.
W 42 St. — E 42 St.
W 34 St. — E 34 St.
W 23 St. — E 23 St.

Queensborough Br.

Queens - Midtown Tun.

Lincoln Tunnel

EAST RIVER

11 Ave.

10 Ave.

9 Ave.

8 Ave.

7 Ave.

6 Ave.

5 Ave.

Madison

Park

Lexington

3 Ave.

2 Ave.

1 Ave.

Ave. A

FDR Drive

⑤ ⑥ ⑦ ② ① ④ ③ ⑨

W 14 St.

Greenwich

Hudson

7 Ave S.

Bleecker

Bowery

Houston

Delancey

Spring

East Broadway

Williamsburg Br.

Canal

Broadway

Holland Tunnel

HUDSON RIVER

Chambers

Manhattan Br.

Brooklyn Br.

Fulton

Wall

St. Marks Pl.

E 14 St.

Brooklyn Battery Tunnel

david yeadon ©

1 Bolton's
43 E.8th St./475-6626 and other locations

A family of outlets serious about savings, but like most discounters, not about much else. Thar's gold in them there racks if you don't mind prospecting for labelless designer fashions in the foray.

2 Emotional Outlet
91 7th Ave. (at W.16th St.)/206-7750 and other locations

Offers amenities, like a sip of coffee or wine and newspapers for the bored husband or boyfriend. The styles here are trendier and younger than other fashion discounters, and they don't go over size 14.

3 First Class
117 Orchard St. (off Delancey St.)/475-8147

If you're in the market for price-slashed designer sportswear (albeit with limited inventory) then this is the place. While you're in the neighborhood (the Lower East Side) check out all the other discounters: from white sales and men's underwear to pickles and prayer shawls, and kid's wear in-between.

4 Friedlich, Inc.
196 Orchard St. (off Houston St.)/254-8899

A real Lower East Side bargain basement, short on tempers and amenities, long on savings and casualwear imports from Italy and France.

5 Labels for Less
1116 Third Ave. (at E.65th St.)/628-1100 and other locations

The discounts here are steady, around 20%. Harvé Bernard and Calvin Klein are well-repped, mostly in separates. Plenty of jeans and big knit tops, too.

Loehmann's
9 Fordham Rd. The Bronx/295-4100 and other locations

This notable non-Manhattan institution is the most habit forming and bargain-worthy of the lot. Go weekly for the best finds. Definitely a tribal rite of J.A.P.s and other idiosyncratic royals.

6 New Store
289 7th Ave. (bet. W.26th & W.27th Sts.)/741-1077

Low-priced silk blouses and cashmere tops are the specialty in this close-to-midtown apparel shop.

7 S&W
165 W.26th St. (bet. 6th & 7th Aves.)/924-6656 and others

Another discounter who has been around forever, offering excellent and varied selection of dresses with high necks and longer sleeves than you might find in other shops, and a heavy emphasis on American designers with matching accessories. Up to 50% off at times.

8 Spitzer's Corner Store
101 Rivington St. (at Ludlow St.)/477-4088
156 Orchard St. (at Rivington St.)/473-1515

Yet one more Lower East Side institution on the Lower East Side. Jam-packed with hot styles for juniors—suits, sportswear, casuals, sweats, dresses and day-to-evening wear in the petites to 14.

9 Syms
45 Park Pl. (bet. Church St. & W. Broadway)/791-1199 and many other locations

Sy is right. An educated consumer is his best customer. Everything is here—larger sizes for men, women and kids, including outerwear, linens, accessories and more, but you have to know your merch to appreciate the bargains.

WOMEN'S HIGH FASHION AND DESIGNER SHOPS

1 Adolpho
36 E.57th St. /688-4410

He's the one for "Reagan Red," and all those copycat frocks worn at press conferences to attract Ronnie's attention; Nancy considers him indispensable, as do other women with large allowances. Appointments are usually necessary.

2 Chanel
5 E.57th St./355-5050

No one should be without something special from here—but of course, you know that already and you'll find these treasures at other city stores, too.

Charivari *see MEN'S HIGH FASHION*

3 Emmanuel Ungaro
803 Madison Ave. (at E.68th St.)/249-4090

The fabrics are impeccable, and his line is the epitome of refined taste. The sales clerks wear his classic, unobtrusive creations and look smarter than most of the clientele.

4 Givenchy Boutique
954 Madison Ave. (at E.75th St.)/772-1040

Everything you've heard is true; it really is that rarified here. The evening wear is guarded (literally) like priceless booty, and tags frighten the faint of heart. But for those who can afford it, the service is superb.

5 Martha
475 Park Ave. (at E.58th St.)/753-1511
Trump Tower, 725 5th Ave. (at E.56th St.)/826-8855

Her parlors resemble all those elegant dress emporia depicted in the movies: solicitous saleswomen with "I have just the thing" on their lips sweep in and out of the showroom, cradling outfits like new-born babies. All the major labels are here for major pocketbooks.

6 Missoni
Westbury Hotel/836 Madison Ave. (at E.69th St.)/517-9339

Men can prospect here too; this distinctive collection of knits (including scarfs, sweaters and other accessories) holds delightful surprises for them, as well as their loved ones.

Ralph Lauren/Polo *see MEN'S HIGH FASHION*

7 Sonia Rykiel Boutique
792 Madison Ave. (at E.67th St.)/744-0880

Another must for devotees of fine knits. Admirers of her dress collection are legion, too.

8 Saint Laurent; Rive Gauche Boutique
855 Madison Ave. (at E.71st St.)/988-3821

Let's dispel the misconception about his name first: Rive Gauche means Left Bank (guess where the Paris boutique is). There's nothing awkward or tasteless about this shop; the master has never lost his touch or grip on imagination. To paraphrase The Commodore, if you ask have to ask how much, you can't afford it.

9 Valentino
825 Madison (bet. E.68th & E.69th Sts.)/772-6969

Jackie Kennedy anointed this Italian designer during her 60's Camelot days, and his staying power is impressive (his refusal to jump to trendy statements probably has a lot to do with it). Shopping here means never having to say you're sorry.

ADULT EDUCATION PROGRAMS

david yeadon ©

Note: Many high schools and colleges in your area offer adult education courses. Call, ask for the department and request a catalogue of courses. They'll all be happy to oblige.

The City University of New York
With branches all over the 5 boroughs and 6 senior institutions: Baruch, Brooklyn, City, Hunter, Lehmann and Queens, as well as the Graduate Center on W.42nd St. These colleges and their sister institutions, the community colleges, should not be ignored as THE absolute NY resource for adult education programs. *see FREE ACADEMIC ACTIVITIES*

Columbia U. School of General Studies
Lewisohn Hall/W.116th St. at Broadway/280-2752
Why not journey uptown to this bastion of liberal learning and see how people from all walks of life, with and without degrees, are continuing to enrich themselves. Day and evening courses are available for credit or not, in every humanistic and applied field.

1 Discovery Center
245 W.72nd St. (bet. Broadway & West End Ave.)/877-0677
The address and the glossy brochure reveal the prime objective—capturing the minds and hearts of the yuppies. Like the Learning Annex, they aim to enlighten and entertain. There are networking parties and biking at Club Getaway, et al. If you're an expert in anything esoteric, volunteer to teach your own class. They love variety.

2 Fordham University at Lincoln Center
113 W.60th St. (bet. Columbus & 10th Aves.)/841-5210
The Excell program grants degree credits for what you've learned in life, and New Yorkers learn a heck of a lot—fast!

3 The Learning Annex
2330 Broadway (bet. W.84 & W.85th Sts.)/769-0600
You've seen their brochures all over town, packed with dozens of courses of a practical or social nature. (Yes, there are singles who attend solely to prospect, but that's just one of the appeals.) They cut a wide swath from origami to the occult, from computer programming to car buying and the culinary arts. If nothing else, the catalogue makes great subway reading.

4 The New School
66 W.12th St./741-5620
Former ambassadors teach about foreign policy, ad agency heads teach advertising and marketing courses, famous artists teach applied arts, and producers discuss contemporary films. There are over 1700 choices in a wide range of career-enhancing, credit-generating (or non- credit generating)and fun classes. An experience that satisfies and looks good on any resume.

5 New York U. School of Continuing Education
Washington Square Campus/505-0467
This is the downtown answer to their rival farther north. Most classes meet at night, and accredited courses are outnumbered by personal enrichment offerings.

6 Stuyvesant Adult Center
Stuyvesant High School
345 E.15th St. (bet. 1st & 2nd Aves.)/254-2890
Everything from antiques to yoga to self-help courses and extensive English as a Second Language programs; the high school equivalency curriculum is a model for others and the senior citizens offerings are innovative. And it's all so inexpensive thanks to the Board of Education.

CHILDREN'S LEARNING CENTERS

1 Children's Book Council
67 Irving Pl. (bet. E.18th & E.19th Sts.)/254-2666

In an age of rampant illiteracy, this wonderful repository of new, old and classic childrens' books should not be missed by parents or teachers.

2 Claremont Riding Academy
175 W.89th St. (bet. Columbus & Amsterdam Aves.)/724-5100

What red-blooded American child doesn't want to gallop on horseback now and then? (Some things never change, thank goodness!) Here's the place to take those who do for safe and thorough instruction, first in their indoor ring and then in Central Park.

3 Cooking for Kids
Hotel Intercontinental
111 E.48th St. (at Park Ave.)/755-5900, ext. 228

No, we're not promoting juvenile hostelry management, just a practical course in cooking dinners and other treats, especially for those whose parents have to work late and don't always get home in time to put supper on the table. Ease your guilt with Saturday classes for the kids.

The Gwendolyn Brown Computer School
P.S. 180/370 W.120th St./678-2925

Cathi Dean, the administrator of this unique institution, notes that Gwendolyn Brown, who founded the school in 1983 and died in 1986, believed programming is a tool to build children's self-confidence in problem solving. Tuition-free and part of the NYC Board of Education, students are recruited from public, private and parochial schools all over the city. They are taught to create their own LOGO language software on Apples, Ataris and IBMs. Some have even synthesized music on their PC's. So get a head start on your child's future and check it out.

4 Manhattan Childrens' Museum
314 W.54th St. (bet. 8th & 9th Aves.)/765-5904

This is the only museum on the island devoted entirely to children. Lend ears and eyes to participatory exhibits and programs here in art, theatre, science and nature. There are special Saturday workshops, too.

5 The Metropolitan Museum of Art
5th Ave. at E.82nd St./570-3961

The Division of Educational Services has replaced the Junior Met program with a top-flight slate of free classes for high school kids. Scheduled for after school and on weekends, the curriculum includes art history, iconography of major works, and fine arts classes for aspiring masters. The collections and special exhibits are used as resources and focal points, and more than one student has arranged classroom credits for efforts here.

6 Weist-Barron School of TV
35 W.45th St./840-7025

This is the oldest training ground in town for budding video thespians, and it's still the best. If your heirs (or you) are aiming for fame and fortune in commercials, soaps or sitcoms, take some of these on-camera classes. Many of the teachers are working actors themselves, and impart practical, as well as technical, advice.

CULTURAL MUSIC CENTERS

1 Bloomingdale House of Music
323 W.108th St. (bet. Broadway & Riverside Dr.)/663-6021
A cozy townhouse, appropriately devoted to chamber music which, after all, was born in such environs and continues to sound best in these intimate surroundings.

Brooklyn Academy of Music
30 Lafayette St. (Brooklyn)/718-636-4100
"BAM" deserves more respectful attention, hence its inclusion here. Facilities include a 2100 seat opera house, the half-size Helen Carey Playhouse, and a very versatile rehearsal/experimental space. International stars and companies still play here. . .we wish they'd try again with repertory theater.

2 Carnegie Hall
154 W.57th St. (off 7th Ave.)/247-7800/903-9750/581-5933
Arguably the most famous concert stage in the world, and as the old joke goes, the only way to get here is still practice, practice, practice. We loved her before the facelift, now she's even more glorious. As long as she stands, she'll remain an apotheosis for every dimension of music, from Beethoven to The Beatles to Tony Bennett and Ole Blue Eyes. Some freebies, too!

3 City Center
131 W.55th St. (bet. 6th and 7th Aves.)/246-8989
A noble, if eccentric-looking, theatre that's thankfully very rarely dark. Many ballet companies, like the Joffrey, Alvin Ailey and Paul Taylor troupes, perform here with regularity, not to mention solo artists like Itzhak Perlman. There is also a laudable tradition of reviving America's classic musicals, this nation's most enduring legacy to the world's dramaturgy.

4 Merkin Concert Hall
Abraham Goodman House
129 W.67th St. (bet. Central Park West & Columbus Ave./362-8719
A warm, modest performance space of recent vintage. The trim auditorium seats 450 and has a pleasing collegiate feel, enhanced by the presence of so many students. They maintain warm relations with all the city's music schools, allowing their novitiates in free or on discounts. Up-and-coming solo artists are the rule, a policy worthy of applause.

5 Lincoln Center For the Performing Arts
Broadway at W. 65th St./877-2011
This magnificent amalgam of entities and edifices is probably the world's finest cultural seat. Here under one banner are Alice Tully Hall, Juilliard School, Metropolitan Opera House, Avery Fischer Hall and The New York State Theatre. Here you can thrill to Bernstein, Pavarotti and Martha Graham. Here you can gaze at such ornaments as Henry Moore's reclining figure, Chagall's murals, and for a brief, sunlit moment, rise above our destructive impulses and claim the part of ourselves that is eternal. Best of all, they offer a remarkable range of free events and concerts.

6 Town Hall
123 W.43rd St. (bet. 6th & 7th Aves.)/840-2824
In comparison to most of the others on this roster, this auditorium seems rather drab, even lonely. While it's not the mecca it was generations ago, you can still attend some intriguing events here. Bravo the famous legend carved upon its face.

FREE ACADEMIC ACTIVITIES

david yeadon ©

Note: The vast range and volume of free and low cost public lectures, films, concerts and other activities at the city's academic institutions boggle the mind. Call the following and obtain monthly, seasonal and semester listings of events. You'll never have a dull night again. see other freebie listings: INDOOR CONCERTS, INDOOR ACTIVITIES and also ADULT EDUCATION

Barnard College
606 W.120th St. (at Broadway)/280-2096
Films, drama, music, Thurs. lectures and seasonal 'festivals.'

1 Baruch College (CUNY)
17 Lexington Ave. (at E.23rd St.)/725-3000
The U.S.A.'s largest business school: free exhibits, concerts, lectures, theatre.

City College (CUNY)
W.131st-W.140th Sts. (bet. St. Nicholas Terr. & Amsterdam Ave.)/690-5310
Unusually appealing campus in an odd and old location; the calendar of free events is a must. (This is CUNY's oldest unit.)

Columbia University
W.115th-W.120th St. (bet. Broadway & Amsterdam Ave.)/280-2845/4771
The mother of all Ivy Leaguers offering countless free activities—a fantastic resource.

Cooper Union *see FREE INDOOR ACTIVITIES*

2 Fordham University
Lincoln Center (W.60th St. and Amsterdam Ave.)/841-5100/5360/5133
Modern humanities center, excellent exhibits, concerts & lectures.

3 Hunter College (CUNY)
E.68th St. (bet. Lexington & Park Aves.)/772-4000
Lectures 772-4085, films 570-5599, theatre 570-5108.

4 Manhattan Community College (CUNY)
199 Chambers St. (at Greenwich St.)/618-1000
Impressive TriBeCa campus; lectures: 618-1605; performances: 618-1443.

Marymount Manhattan College
221 E.71st St. (bet. 2nd & 3rd Aves.)/472-3800
Independent liberal arts college for women offering a wide range of activities—exhibits, theatre, lectures and workshops.

5 New York University
Washington Square at W.4th St./598-1212/2451
Great liberal institution in the Village; "NYU Scene" gives details of vast range of free events.

7 Pace University
Civic Center Campus (east of City Hall)/488-1200,1360-1617
Excellent business courses, free "lunch & learn" lectures, films & concerts.

8 Third Street Music School Settlement
233 E.11th St. (bet. 2nd & 3rd Aves.)/777-3240
Free faculty concerts usually on Tuesdays & Thursdays at 7:30, plus other special events.

Yeshiva University
Amsterdam Ave. at W.185th St./960-5288
Excellent museum exhibits (960-5390)and free lectures on Judaic subjects.

FREE INDOOR CONCERTS

E 110 St.
E 106 St.
W 106 St.
E 96 St.
W 96 St.
West End Ave.
Riverside Dr.
Columbus
Amsterdam
Broadway
West End Ave.
Central Park West
W 86 St.
Central Park
5 Ave.
Madison
Park
Lexington
3 Ave.
2 Ave.
1 Ave.
York Ave.
E 86 St.
W 79 St.
E 79 St.
W 72 St.
CENTRAL PARK
E 72 St.
Broadway
W 65 St.
E 65 St.
W 59 St.
E 59 St.
Queensborough Br.
W 57 St.
E 57 St.
W 50 St.
E 50 St.
W 42 St.
E 42 St.
Queens - Midtown Tun.
Lincoln Tunnel
W 34 St.
E 34 St.
11 Ave.
W 23 St.
E 23 St.
EAST RIVER
10 Ave.
9 Ave.
8 Ave.
7 Ave.
6 Ave.
5 Ave.
Madison
Park
Lexington
3 Ave.
2 Ave.
1 Ave.
F.D.R. Drive
W 14 St.
E 14 St.
Ave. A
Greenwich
St. Marks Pl.
HUDSON
7 Ave. S.
Hudson
Bleecker
Bowery
Houston
Spring
Delancey
Williamsburg Br.
Holland Tunnel
Canal
Broadway
East Broadway
RIVER
Chambers
Manhattan Br.
Brooklyn Br.
Fulton
Wall
Brooklyn Battery Tunnel

david yeadon ©

1 Bloomingdale House of Music/ *323 W.108th St. (bet. Broadway & Riverside Dr.)/663-6021*
Usually Wednesdays at 8 p.m.; also inexpensive concerts on Fridays and Sundays.

Carnegie Hall *see CULTURAL MUSIC CENTERS*

Citicorp Center *see ATRIUMS*

Columbia University/ *St. Paul's Chapel/W.117th St. & Amsterdam Ave./280-5113*
Thursday noon organ recitals. May-June: Thursday Bach concerts at 8 p.m.

Donnell Library *see LIBRARIES*

2 Frick Collection/ *1 E.70th St./288-0700*
Well worth the ticket request process for concerts Sundays at 5 and Wednesdays at 5:30

Galleria *see ATRIUMS*

3 Abraham Goodman House/ *129 W.67th St. (at Broadway)/362-8060*
An array of free and low-cost concerts by students and faculty.

Lincoln Center for the Performing Arts *see CULTURAL MUSIC CENTERS*

4 Maison Française (NYU)/ *16 Washington Mews (off University Pl.)/598-2161*
Excellent free concerts on the third Sunday of the month at 3 p.m. Oct.-May. Reserve.

Manhattan School of Music/ *W.122 St. at Broadway/749-2802*
An almost daily array of free concerts.

5 Mannes College of Music/ *150 W.85th St. (bet. Columbus & Amsterdam Aves.)/580-0210*
Usually Monday-Friday at 8 p.m., all year long.

6 Museum of The City of New York/ *5th Ave. at E.103rd St./534-1672*
Occasional Sunday 3 p.m. concerts and low-fee entertainments at 5 p.m.

Riverside Church/ *490 Riverside Dr. (at W.122nd St.)/222-5900*
Summer Tuesday 6 p.m. concerts, Sunday afternoon recitals and carillion concerts at Saturday noon and Sundays at 3 p.m.

Theodore Roosevelt's Birthplace *see OVERLOOKED MUSEUMS II*

7 St. Patrick's Cathedral/ *5th Ave. at E.50th St./753-2261*
Sunday organ recitals at 4:30 p.m.

8 St. Peter's Church/ *Citicorp Center/Lexington at E.54th St./935-2200*
Beloved jazz vespers on Sundays at 5; Jazz on Wednesdays at noon, Oct.-June.

9 Symphony Space/ *Broadway at W.95th St./864-1414*
Famous "wall-to-wall" 12 hour concerts.

0 WNCN Radio/ *1180 6th Ave. (bet. W.46th & W.47th Sts.)/730-9626*
Excellent live concerts Tuesdays at 8 p.m. Reservations.

*Note: The range of regularly scheduled free concerts confirms New York as the world's #1 showcase city. **Always call ahead for details and reservations.***

HOUSES OF WORSHIP

david yeadon ©

1 The Cathedral of St. John the Divine
Amsterdam Ave. at 112th St./316-7540/662-2133 (events)
Since 1892, generations of stonecutters have been dressing stones in the medieval European tradition for this grand Gothic masterpiece. When finished, it will be the world's largest Christian house of worship, and meanwhile, its soaring grace impresses, and its tours and adult education programs are stimulating. *see FREE GUIDED TOURS*

2 The Central Synagogue, 1868
652 Lexington Ave. (at E.55th St.)/838-5122
This is the synagogue of Congregation Ahavath Chesed (lovers of acts of kindness) which was founded in 1842 and moved four times before resting here, and becoming the oldest continuously-used synagogue in town. Moorish designs became very popular for synagogue architecture in the 19th century, and this is a fine example of the genre. Call for tour details.

3 The Little Church Around the Corner
Church of the Transfiguration/1 E.29th St. (at 5th Ave.)/684-6770
Over a hundred years ago, some priggish pastor refused to bury a destitute actor, and his snooty referral became the unofficial name of this Episcopal parish. Its devotion to and popularity with the Broadway crowd endures and the intimate mood and tranquil garden delight the world-weary.

4 Marble Collegiate Church
272 5th Ave. (at 29th St.)/686-2770
Followers of the powerful proponent of positive thinking, Dr. Norman Vincent Peale, still hold forth here on Sunday mornings, and the congregation departs, unloaded and uplifted.

Riverside Church
490 Riverside Dr. (at W.122nd St.)/222-5900
This is one more gift from the Rockefellers—an interdenominational edifice with the world's largest carillion and bell,and famed clergy rabble-rouser, William Sloane Coffin. It also offers a stimulating array of free cultural and intellectual programs.

5 St. Bartholomew's
Park Ave. & E.50th St./751-1616
This Byzantine jewelbox is a notable Park Ave. landmark and may the good Lord preserve her community house from the hi-rise philistines. Also provides a wide range of cultural freebies.

6 St. Marks In the Bowery
131 E.10th St. (at 2nd Ave.)/674-6377
In the heart of this old New York district, sitting on the site of Peter Stuyvesant's 1609 chapel, (he still restlessly tosses about the ancient cemetery). Recent post-fire renovations have not disrupted its character, and it still offers a wide variety of poetry readings and much more.

7 St. Patrick's Cathedral, 1858-74
5th Ave. (at 50th St.)/753-2261
A sublime, if slightly complacent, Gothic hybrid and the city's most famous house of worship. Popes Paul and John Paul II have led masses here and the good Cardinal O'Connor can always be counted on to keep the faith alive,embroiled in controversy with his touch of humor and hubris.

Trinity Church/*see HISTORIC LANDMARKS*

LIBRARIES

American Museum of Natural History *see*
MAJOR MUSEUMS

1 Central Research Branch, The New York Public Library
5th Ave. and W.42nd St./869-8089/221-7676 for calendar of events
Not only NY's best, but quite possibly the world's supreme depository of the written world (5 million books and 12 million periodicals) all housed in a Beaux Arts masterpiece guarded by Patience and Fortitude—the two ubiquitous lions. Also visit the **Mid-Manhattan** branch across the street on 5th & 40th, which is the largest circulation library in town.

2 Donnell Library
20 W.53rd St. (off 5th Ave.)/621-0600/0618
In addition to a massive circulation collection, they also offer free concerts, poetry readings, theatre performances, films, book seminars and showcase entertainments—all of high quality.

3 Jefferson Market Library
425 6th Ave. (at W.10th St.)/243-4334
This novel Victorian-Gothic fantasy of a library contains an excellent collection and offers regular lectures, workshops, poetry readings, drama, craft demonstrations and children's events. A vibrant neighborhood hub.

4 The Library and Museum of Performing Arts
Lincoln Center at W.66th St./870-1600/1630
World's largest collection of manuscripts and memorabilia related to dance, theatre, opera and music, plus research, records and videos, exhibitions and regular free performances every day. An outstanding resource.

5 New York Academy of Medicine
2 E.103rd St. (off 5th Ave.)/876-8200
Everything you'll ever need to know about medicine and the medical sciences, plus helpful staff and occasional lectures.

6 N.Y. Genealogical & Biographical Society
122 E.58th St. (bet. Park & Lexington Aves.)/755-8582
Charming reading room setting where you can root out your ancestors in comfort, using one of 70,000 volumes and friendly librarian assistance (occasional small fee).

7 New York Historical Society
170 Central Park West (bet. W.76th & W.77th Sts.)/873-3400
Fascinating museum which is a repository of American history archives as well as acting as a mini-Smithsonian for City stuff.

8 New York Society Library
53 E.79th St. (bet. Park & Madison Aves./288-6900
The city's oldest membership library, founded in 1754, and a true gem, housed in a Beaux Arts townhouse. Over 200,000 volumes in a collection spanning biography, travel, art and literature are available to visitors in the reading room.

Schomburg Center
515 Lenox Ave. (at E.135th St.)/862-4000
A major center for the study of Black culture with consoles for historical recordings and videos, gallery exhibits, sculpture garden and occasional lectures and concerts.

9 YIVO (Institute for Jewish Research)
1048 5th Ave. (at E.86th St.)/535-6700
The Vanderbilt Mansion now houses the most extensive historical collections of Yiddish masterworks and genealogical archives in the post-WWII universe. Unique.

POETRY READING CENTERS

david yeadon ©

Please excuse a little levity in our playful praise of poetic pantheons.

1 Academy of American Poets
177 E.87th St. (bet. Lexington and 3rd Aves.)/427-5665
For 53 years, they've invited the best/Frost, Pound and cummings and all of the rest/To read and to write, even philosophize/in hope they might win a ten-thousand buck prize./If you call for the name, the locale and the time/you'll listen to works that are fairly sublime.

2 Back Fence
155 Bleecker St. (at Thompson St.)/475-9221
4:30 on Sundays this folk-rock song club/allows budding bards undeterred if they flub/to try out their lines on the elbowing throng./With so many critics how can they go wrong?

3 Ear Inn
326 Spring St. (bet. Greenwich & Washington Sts.)/226-9060
On non-summer Saturdays inside this place/the published and un get equivalent grace./It is funky and fun in this dim-lit bistro./If you slumber while listening, no one will know.

4 Hudson Guild
441 W.26th St. (bet. 9th & 10th Aves.)/760-9800
On the second Thursday/October through May/from 7 - 9 p.m., their brochures say/a state funded program bids poet fans enter/this quite well regarded and run resource center.

5 The New York Public Library
5th Ave and W.42nd St./930-0855
Patience and Fortitude, lions of pride/know that there's much more than books here inside./Phone for the free program calendar manual./It lists all the readings and such that are annual.

6 The 92nd Street Y
1395 Lexington Ave. (at E.92nd St.)/427-4410
Poets and actors converge at this matrix/to read and interpret and show us their best tricks./Greats and upcoming ones share center stage/all of them talented, all of them sage.

7 Poetry Project at St. Marks
10th St. and 2nd Ave./674-0910/6377
The beats used to bleat on this church's home turf/thank god the building has had a rebirth!/workshops and showcases rule the roost here/on Monday and Wednesday nights, nearly all year/go read you own verse and let them respond/could be you're the big fish in Manhattan's pond.

8 Poetry Society of America
National Arts Club
15 Gramercy Park So. (on E.20th St.)/254-9628
An elegant enclave since 19 and 10/they're soon to begin public readings again./Call and be put on the house mailing list/P.S. their huge library shouldn't be missed.

9 Womanbooks
201 W.92nd St. (at Amsterdam Ave.)/873-4121
There once were some feminist thinkers/whose poems were not clinkers/they have readings here that are chauvinist clear/for their credo is "Sexists are stinkers!"

0 The Writer's Voice
YMCA Arts Center
5 W.63rd St. (off Central Park West)/787-6557
October, November, December/and then March and April and May/are the months they would have you remember/for the poem nights on Wed. and Friday.

REVIVAL MOVIE HOUSES

david yeadon ©

1 The Bleecker St. Cinema
144 Bleecker St. (bet. Thompson & LaGuardia)/674-2560
An intimate little bandbox, fond of premiering rarities and esoterica, too. A culture-chic touchstone, and site of scenes in some movies, too. . .like "Desperately Seeking Susan."

2 Carnegie Hall Cinema
7th Ave. at W.57th St./757-2131
Fond of European flicks and thematic series. Savor its lovely, ornate interior, evocative of 19th century opera houses.

3 Cinema Village
22 E.12th St./924-3363
Like the late-lamented Hollywood Twin (now a first-run house), this screen features predominantly American films.

4 The Regency
Broadway at W.67th St./724-3700
Our favorite among this vanishing breed. Its month-long series are really celebrations of various studios' and artists' best. Long may she wave.

5 Thalia
Broadway at W.95th St./222-3370
Always worth a trip, even if you didn't check the listings first. They like short subjects, too.

6 Thalia Screen
15 Vandam St. (west of 6th Ave.)/675-0498
A second branch of **Thalia** tucked away in this quiet part of town with a penchant for subtitled art films and revivals. If you're a strict revivalist, call first.

7 Theatre 80 St. Marks
80 St. Marks Pl. (at Ave. A)/254-7400
Bless 'em, they love a mixed bag here. Robin Hood one day, The Thin Man the next. . .but the place reeks of film history and fouder Howard Otway's love of the silver screen.

HEALTH CLUBS

1 Apple Health and Sports Clubs
88 Fulton St., (bet. South St. and Broadway)/227-7450
and other locations
These well-appointed facilities have a business posture as sleek and no-nonsense as their most dedicated members. Wall Streeters don't socialize here. . .they exercise.

2 Cardio-Fitness Centers
79 Maiden Lane (bet. William & Gold Sts.)/943-1510
130 E.52nd St. (bet. Park & Lexington Aves.)/838-4570
As one might expect, these shops are devoted to keeping the corporate fast-tracker running from stress and heart trouble. Their staffers are as tenacious as skilled pro coaches.

3 Club 29
155 E.29th St. (bet. Lexington & 3rd Aves.)/679-2299
You can work out and quite possibly make out here, considering the nearly 50-50 ratio between the sexes, the lounge, the frequent parties, and the romantic vistas from the roof. Oh yes, and they have plenty of fitness equipment, too.

4 Executive Fitness Center
At The Vista International Hotel
3 World Trade Center/466-9266
Non-guests pay a premium, but for those who can afford the fee it's surely worth it. The pool and the track are bigger than most, and the medically based, personally designed workouts rival the hi-tech regimens at the Cardio-Fitness outposts.

5 Manhattan Plaza Health Club
484 W.43rd St. (at 10th Ave.)/563-7001
Atop the twin-towered artists' colony, this may be the most attractive club in terms of decor and fee, pool and excellent tennis courts.

6 New York Health and Racquet Clubs
1433 York Ave. (at E.76th St.)/737-6666
and other locations
The progenitors of marketing to an upscale clientele and worthy of their rarified image. Membership includes plenty of extras, implicit and ex. Many clients rely on this venerable institution for social, as well as physical fitness.

7 Paris Health Club
752 West End Ave. (at W.96th St.)/749-3500
A spiritual relation to Manhattan Plaza, with a crackerjack staff. Check out the class offerings.

8 Pineapple Broadway
599 Broadway (at Houston St.)/219-8860
Fascinating mix of dance and aerobic classes (150 different varieties, including belly-dancing) plus gym for serious SoHo types with fitness and form in mind. A novel London import by Debbie Moore.

9 Sports Training Institute
239 E.49th St. (at 3rd Ave.)/752-7111
Originally for the professionals (some still come), this one's for those who like being shepherded; everyone works out by appointment with a trainer.

0 The Vertical Club
330 E.61st St. at The 59th St. Bridge Ramp/355-5100
A ritzy East Side establishment; this one's dressed as a gym with all the elaborate trimmings, but it's really the singles bar of the '80s.

JOGGING ROUTES

david yeadon ©

1 The Brooklyn Bridge
Access from Manhattan via William St. at Municipal Bldg.; access from Brooklyn at Tillary St.
During the last transit strike, many sedentary NYorkers discovered what joggers always knew: that this "cathedral" of bridges is prime pedestrian water-crossing territory. The view, the breezes, the bridge itself and its historical aura (and awesome engineering) truly enhance the joy of jogging.

2 Central Park
59-110th Sts. (bet. 5th Ave. and Central Park West)
Of course you can run literally everywhere here, but most joggers choose the East and West drives and the paths around the reservoir (famous for its star-studded faces and "race-a-celeb" contests). The high fence around the water is, unfortunately, a necessity, or so they say.

3 East River Promenade
From South Ferry to E.125th St. (with breaks in-between)
Run all the way to Randall's Island, if you wish (you'll take a few detours), but there are plenty of benches along the way, should you need a breather. But don't try it rush hours on Mondays through Fridays—the traffic pollution will wreck your lungs. The best stretch is John Finley Walk, from E.81st to Gracie Mansion and Carl Schurz Park.

Fort Tryon Park
Fort Washington Ave./end of Fort Washington Ave. in Washington Heights
Secluded, hilly, leafy, and very romantic, but a difficult run—the hills here are steep. **The Cloisters Museum** is a lovely diversion, the autumn season especially impressive, and the area possibly the most peaceful in town.
see MAJOR MUSEUMS

Inwood Hill Park
Dyckman St. and Spuyten Duyvil Creek
The nothernmost tip of the Island, and a trek from midtown, but this former haunt of cave-dwelling Native Americans will provide a good workout along a series of woodland hills and dales. If you're lonely, bring a friend.

4 Riverside Park
W.72nd St. to The George Washington Bridge
Somewhat hilly and quite European in flavor; farther up, Riverside Drive takes on the flavor of Paris, which the more spartan harriers seem to appreciate. The Hudson is a hypnotically soothing background, especially in winter, but beware those biting breezes.

5 Roosevelt Island
By aerial tram from E.59th St. & 2nd Ave. or by car from Queens
The silence at the lovely riverside pausing places and the restored **Blackwell Farmhouse** create an otherworldly atmosphere, even the tall towers have a friendly feel along the curling main street. Well worth the trip.

6 Washington Square Park
The heart of Greenwich Village at the southern end of 5th Ave.
Plenty of people-watching, so watch out for obstacles that may interfere with the short half-mile run around one of the city's most delightful spaces. Four circuits are considered starter level, but the trick is to keep running despite the distractions, (no matter how strange!)

183

THE BEST Y'S

McBurney YMCA
215 W.23rd St. (bet. 7th & 8th Aves.)/741-9210/741-9226 (for overnight accomodation)

Prior to the effects of a five-year renovation (which is now almost finished), members had to make do with overcrowded workouts. No longer. It's clean and comfy here now, even though the shell of these nine floors was built in 1904. The gym, with full basketball court, has a pleasing high school air about it and the pool (24" x 48") and the track (1/20th of a mile) are larger than most. Check out the view from the sundeck.

The 92nd St. Y (M-WHA)
1395 Lexington Ave. (at E. 92nd St.)/427-6000

This bustling, thriving place also serves as the city's Jewish community center, and offers myriads of free services to all city residents. The film series and lectures, the classical concerts, are all top notch. The cultural programs stress the vast diversities of Jewish life, and they have pioneered in such subjects as the Holocaust and served as a forum for debate on seminal Jewish issues. Members are treated even better, and the building is in excellent shape with a wonderful theatre and side rooms. . .all marble and beautiful woodwork. They have more to give than most people can accept.

The Sloane House YMCA
356 W.34th St. (bet. 8th & 9th Aves.)/760-5850

Even callow colleagues from Actors Equity agree that this place isn't at all bad. That's not surprising. The rates are reasonable in this old monolith, and there's a pretty fair cafeteria and a laundry to go with the 1500 rooms. They've even got Nautilus machines!

The Vanderbilt Y
224 E.47th St.(off Vanderbilt Ave.)/755-2410

A good deal plusher than the others, as the address would suggest. Like Sloane House, it's a combination boarding house/youth hostel with 400 rooms, eating facilities and a laundromat. They also have safe deposit boxes and a gift shop. (Can you believe it? You thought Y's were just joints where working stiffs got together to sweat!) It's all air-conditioned, too!

West Side YMCA
5 W.63rd St./787-4400

They're renowned for the top-notch shape-up program, but you can set up housekeeping here too. Perks include a free fitness evaluation in a private spa atmosphere. Some of the ornate trimmings include a posh lobby and a pool area that shows off handpainted tiles donated by the King of pre-Franco Spain in the '30s. (Now, that's a great cocktail party trivia question!) The size of the membership rolls, the range of programs and the equipment inventory are staggering.

The YWCA of New York City
610 Lexington Ave. (bet. E.52nd & E.53rd Sts.)/755-4500

Sorry, guys. This one's for women only. It serves them exceedingly well, too, with conditioning opportunities for every gal—from the most sedentary to the Olympic medalists who might happen to drop by. The membership fee is low, but most of the facilities and group functions levy usage fees. The kids' fencing and gymnastics training here is noteworthy.

ANNUAL FAIRS & FESTIVALS *see also PARADES and FREE OUTDOOR CONCERTS. Call the New York Convention & Visitor's Bureau at 397-8222 or The Parks Department at 755-4100 for details.*

The Chinese New Year
THE FIRST FULL MOON AFTER JAN. 21/Mulberry and Mott Sts. Ten fiery days of firecrackers, frolics, diversions and glorious food.

The Ninth Avenue International Food Festival
THE FIRST WEEKEND AFTER MOTHER'S DAY/From W.38th up to W.57th St. A popular celebration of gastronomic diversity.

St. Anthony Fiesta
LATE MAY/Mulberry St. in Little Italy. One of a series of lively food-and-games festivals, including another St. Anthony Festival in late June; Lady of Pompeii Festival on Cornelia St. in early July; and The Feast of San Gennaro in mid-September.

Washington Square Outdoor Art Exhibit
STARTS THE LAST WEEKEND IN MAY. For three successive week-ends of arts (& crafts) from the so-so to the sublime, and they do it all over again in mid-September.

Museum Mile Festival
THE FIRST OR SECOND TUESDAY IN JUNE/5th Ave. bet. 86th &106th Sts. Cultural extravaganza at all Upper 5th Ave. Museums.

The Fourth of July *see PARADES*

American Crafts Festival
USUALLY EARLY JULY/Lincoln Center. Excellent exhibits plus all the usual diversions.

Festival of the Americas
USUALLY LATE AUGUST/6th Ave. between W.30th & W.50th Sts. One of the most spectacular annual events.

Out of Doors Festival
IN MID-AUGUST/Lincoln Center. Three weeks of outdoor theatre, singing dance, mime—whatever!

The Fifth Avenue Book Fair
USUALLY MID-SEPTEMBER/5th Ave. bet. 48th & 59th Sts. Every-thing to do with books, authors and publishing. Great!

One World Day
EARLY SEPTEMBER/St. Vartan's Cathedral, E.35th St. & 2nd Ave. A moving experience with multinational amusements.

Third Ave. Annual Street Fair
MID-SEPTEMBER/bet. E.68th & E.90th Sts.

52nd St. Fair
MID-SEPTEMBER/bet. 3rd & 8th Aves.

Governor's Island Open House
THE FIRST SUNDAY AFTER LABOR DAY, and sometimes on Armed Forces Weekend in May. An unusual harbor experience and worth the trip.

TAMA Grandparents' Day
MID-SEPTEMBER/3rd Ave., bet. E.14th & E.35th Sts. A mile of country fair pleasures and fleamarkets.

The New York City Marathon
THE LAST SUNDAY IN OCTOBER, 9 a.m./Begins Verrazano Nar-rows Bridge in Staten Island, ends in Central Park

Christmas & Chanukah Celebrations
ALL MONTH LONG. Scores of events throughout the city includ-ing the December 1 lighting of the Christmas tree at Rockefeller Center, and the 5th Avenue Holiday festival, with the Avenue closed for the two Sundays before Christmas.

New Year's Celebrations *see PARADES*

EVENTS TO REMEMBER

Note: For general information and specific dates for sports events (not included here) call the Visitor's Bureau at 397-822 or the Parks Department at 755-4100. For precise information call the following locations:

Jacob Javits Convention Center (JJCC)/216-2000
Lincoln Center (LC)/877-2011
Madison Square Garden (MSG)/564-4400
Also see FAIRS & FESTIVALS/FREE OUTDOOR ENTERTAINMENTS/ FREE OUTDOOR CONCERTS/PARADES

JANUARY

The Ice Capades at MSG/*(LATE)*
The National Boat Show at JJCC/*(MID)*
Winter Antiques Show at the Regiment Armory/*(LATE)*/665-5250

FEBRUARY

International Antiques Show at MSG/*(MID)*
New York City Opera Spring Season at LC/*(LATE through Mar.)*
U.S.A. Track & Field Championships at MSG/*(LATE)*
Westminster Kennel Club Dog Show at MSG/*(LATE)*

MARCH

Ringling Brothers, Barnum & Bailey Circus at MSG *(LATE through May)*

APRIL

International Auto Show at JJCC*(EARLY)*
New York City Ballet Spring Season*(LATE through June)*

JUNE

Basically Bach at LC *(EARLY)*
Big Apple Circus at various locations *(MID through Aug.)*/369-5110

JULY

Mostly Mozart at LC *(EARLY-Aug.)*

AUGUST

Governor's Cup Race at Battery Park City Esplanade *(LATE or EARLY Sept.)*
Harlem Week at various uptown sites *(MID)*/427-7200

SEPTEMBER

Mayor's Cup Schooner Race at Battery Park *(LATE)*/689-9400
New York Film Festival at LC *(MID-Oct.)*

OCTOBER

Fall Antiques Show at Pier 90 *(LATE)*/foot of W.54th St./777-5218
Joffrey Ballet at City Center, 131 W.55th St. (bet. 6th & 7th Aves.) *(MID through Nov.)*/246-8989

NOVEMBER

Christmas Star Show at Hayden Planetarium *(LATE through Jan.)*/873-8828
National Horse Show at MSG (EARLY)
Radio City Christmas Spectacular *(LATE through Jan.)*/757-3100

DECEMBER

Christmas Revels at Symphony Space *(EARLY)/Broadway at W.95th St./864-5400*
Messiah Sing-in at LC (LATE)
National Antiques Show at JJCC *(MID)*
The Nutcracker Ballet at JJCC *(LATE through Dec.)*
WBAI Holiday Crafts Fair *(3 WEEKENDS)/Ferris Booth Hall at Columbia University/279-0707*

FREE GUIDED TOURS

*Note: Tours are occasionally subject to seasonal and other consid-erations by the sponsoring institutions. **Always call in advance** to check details.*

American Museum of Natural History/*873-1300*
see MAJOR MUSEUMS

Cathedral of St. John the Divine/*678-6888*
see HOUSES OF WORSHIP

Columbia University/*280-2845*
see FREE ACADEMIC ACTIVITIES/ADULT EDUCATION/FREE INDOOR CONCERTS

Federal Reserve Bank of New York/*791-6130*
33 Liberty St. (at Nassau St.)
You must call a week in advance, but it's worth it to see all that money being counted and more gold than Fort Knox.

Governor's Island/*668-7255*
Only two open-house tours a year at this quaint and surprising Coast Guard community in the harbor. Sometimes group tours are available.

Grand Central Station *see ATRIUMS*

Library & Museum of the Performing Arts
see LIBRARIES

Metropolitan Museum of Art/*879-5500, 535-7710*
see MAJOR MUSEUMS

New York Public Library at 5th Ave. & 42nd St./*661-7220/340-0849/221-7676 for free calendar of events*
see LIBRARIES/HISTORIC LANDMARKS

New York Stock Exchange *see TOURIST ATTRACTIONS*

Seventh Regiment Armory
Park Ave. (bet. E.66th & E.67th Sts.)
Hidden splendors in a variety of room displays culminating in the outstanding Veteran's Room.

Shapiro's Winery *see FREE INDOOR ACTIVITIES*

United Nations *see FREE INDOOR ACTIVITIES*

Urban Park Rangers/*397-3091/360-8194*
An excellent choice of free park walks.

Whitney Museum of American Art/*570-3600*
see MAJOR MUSEUMS

FREE OUTDOOR CONCERTS

Summer in Manhattan offers a wealth of major cultural events and concerts—all top-notch and all free! See also FREE OUTDOOR ACTIVITIES or call The Visitors' Bureau at 397-8222 or The Parks Department at 755-4100.

Channel Gardens
Rockefeller Center (bet. W.48th & W.51st Sts., bet. 5th & 6th Aves.)/489-4306
'Music for a City Evening' on summer Wednesdays 5-6:30, (plus Tuesday & Thursday noontime concerts in Exxon Park.

Goldman Memorial Band Concerts
at Lincoln Center/867-8290
One of the city's oldest 'freebies' featuring concerts in Lincoln Center's Damrosch Park from late June-August, W,Th,F,Su

Kool Jazz Festival/ *787-2020*
Various city concert locales and often free from late June-early July.

Lincoln Center Out-Of-Doors
see ANNUAL FAIRS & FESTIVALS

Metropolitan Opera Company/ *362-6000*
Free outdoor evening operas in major city parks throughout June.

New York Dance Festival
Delacorte Theatre in Central Park at E.81st St./535-5630
The world of dance from folk to fantasia, usually for one week in early September.

New York Grand Opera/ *245-8837*
Full productions at various city parks, including the Bandshell in Central Park. Throughout July.

The New York Philharmonic/ *580-8700/877-2011*
Unforgettable evenings on Central Park's Great Lawn and in other parks during August.

New York Women's Jazz Festival/ *505-5660*
A week of free and not-so-free concerts at various city locations in mid-June.

Shakespeare in the Park/ *861-PAPP*
The Big One—thousands queue for the free tickets to these splendid Delacorte Theatre productions from late June through September. Indelible.

South Street Seaport/ *669-9400*
Free "Summerpier" jazz & folk concerts usually, Th-Fr at 8 p.m. from Memorial Day to Labor Day.

Summergarden
Museum of Modern Art/11 W.53th St./708-9840
Usually Friday & Saturday 6 p.m. concerts in the museum's beautiful sculpture garden (early July-mid-August.)

Washington Square Music Festival
Washington Square Park/431-1088
Chamber recitals for everyone on Tuesdays at 8 p.m. through July & August.

PARADES

Note: Dates & routes vary from year to year, so call the always dependable Visitor's Bureau at 397-8222 or the Parks Department at 755-4100. For other information on parades contact the local police precinct. Listings are chronological.

St. Patrick's Day Parade/March 17/11 a.m./5th Ave. from 44th-86th Sts./A glorious day, rain or shine, for overindulgences.

Greek Independence Day Parade/Third Sunday in March/1 p.m./5th Ave. from 62nd-79th Sts./Usually starts off calmly, but by late afternoon, it's a fiery festival.

Easter Weekend/Central Park Egg Rolling Contest/Great Lawn/12:30 p.m./Kids galore, scores of wooden eggs and parades.

Easter Parade/Easter Sunday/St. Patrick's Cathedral on 5th Ave. to 59th St./Wonderful bonnets and spring-tinged brouhaha.

Solidarity Day Parade/A Sunday in late April or early May, 11 a.m./5th Ave. from 61st St. to 47th St. to Dag Hammerskjold Plaza/Public support for human rights in USSR. Everyone is invited to march.

Lesbian & Gay Pride Day Parade/Late in June/From Central Park West and W.61st St. down 5th Ave. to Washington Square, down Waverly Pl. to Christopher St./A riotous occasion, whatever your sexual persuasions.

Independence Day/July 4/Harbor Festival in downtown area daytime with fireworks along the Hudson at the Statue of Liberty, moving north at 9 p.m.

Labor Day/First Monday in September. Street Fair on 42nd St. bet. 9th & 10th Aves.

Steuben Day Parade/mid-September/5th Ave. from 61st to 86th St. and then to Yorkville/Boldly Germanic celebrations of Washington's Prussian General, Baron Von Steuben.

Pulaski Day Parade/Oct. 5/5th Ave. & 26th-52nd Sts., east to 3rd Ave.

Columbus Day Parade/Oct. 13/11:30 a.m./5th Ave. & 44th St.-86th St.

Hispanic-Columbus Day Parade/Oct. 12/5th Ave. & 44th St.-72nd St., east to 3rd Ave.

Halloween Parade/Oct. 31/Christopher St. to Washington Square/General insanity with marvelous masques and costumes that goes all night long.

Macy's Thanksgsgiving Day Parade/The last Thursday in November, 9 a.m./From Central Park West & 77th St. to Columbus Circle, down Broadway to Herald Square. The biggest, most exciting, extravagant, professional, kid-oriented parade in the universe!

New Year's Eve Celebration in Times Square
It's not really a parade, but millions throng into Times Square to watch the apple fall and others gallop to Central Park for the Midnight Run and the fireworks. It's the classic New York way to end the old and start the new!

INDEX

INDEX

193

194

199

SUGGESTIONS PLEASE!

A guide of this type needs constant updating and re-evaluation. and so we invite you participate.

Please note any new candidates you consider appropriate for **NEW YORK: The Best Places** *or any inclusions you feel should be removed (with your reasons, if possible.)*

Thank you for your help. Every suggestion will be examined in our efforts to improve next year's edition.

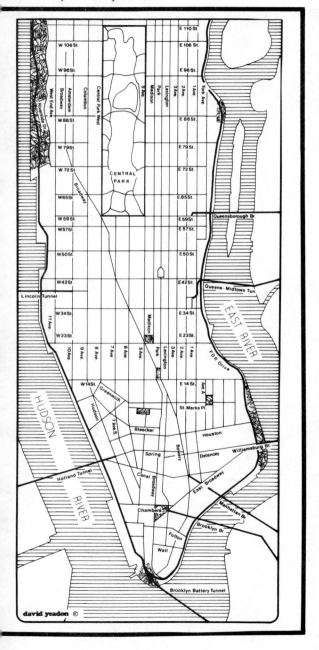

david yeadon ©

NOTES